Tools for Achieving
TQE

Total Quality Education for the World's Best Schools

The Comprehensive Planning and Implementation Guide for School Administrators

Series Editor: **Larry E. Frase**

The authors dedicate this series to the memory of
W. Edwards Deming, 1900-1993

Tools for Achieving TQE

Raymond F. Latta
Carolyn J. Downey

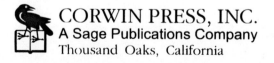
CORWIN PRESS, INC.
A Sage Publications Company
Thousand Oaks, California

For information address:

 Corwin Press, Inc.
A Sage Publications Company
2455 Teller Road
Thousand Oaks, California 91320

SAGE Publications Ltd.
6 Bonhill Street
London EC2A 4PU
United Kingdom

SAGE Publications India Pvt. Ltd.
M-32 Market
Greater Kailash I
New Delhi 110 048 India

Printed in the United States of America

Library of Congress Cataloging-in-Publication Data

Latta, Raymond F.
    Tools for achieving TQE / Raymond F. Latta, Carolyn J. Downey.
        p. cm. — (Total quality education for the world's best
    schools, v. 10)
    Includes bibliographical references.
    ISBN 0-8039-6178-2 (pbk.: alk. paper)
    1. School management and organization—United States. 2. Total
quality management—United States. I. Downey, Carolyn J.
II. Title. III. Series.
LB2805.L337 1994
371.2'00973—dc20   94-9174

94 95 96 97 98 10 9 8 7 6 5 4 3 2 1

Corwin Press Production Editor: Marie Louise Penchoen

✧ ✧

Contents

✧   ✧

Foreword

Many people believe that the most difficult aspect of the quality movement is how to effectively apply the statistical quality tools to educational uses. Terms like "variance," graphs depicting lines of slope, and banks of data can be intimidating, but they need not be. Clarity is what this book is about. In the following pages, Ray Latta and Carolyn Downey provide clear narrative explanations and more than 110 graphics and tables to fully illustrate practical uses of quality tools in helping reduce variance and improve quality. In addition, nine statistical applications are presented in straightforward language, using easy-to-understand terms.

The quality tools and techniques for reducing variance profiled in this book include benchmarking, process diagrams, decision-making grids, cause-and-effect analysis, scatter diagrams, control charts, pareto charts, and force-field analysis. The authors have combined their vast job experience as principals, curriculum directors, assistant superintendents, superintendents, and professors to clearly define each tool and demonstrate its statistical application at four accountability levels: classroom, school, district, and governing board.

The applications of the tools and processes selected by the authors are clearly linked to key quality concepts such as continuous improvement, vision, mission, systems, quality indicators, and the continuous improvement system cycle. The authors capture these key quality concepts in what they term *Continuous*

Quality Improvement (CQI). They define and present CQI as the primary means for attaining *Total Quality Education* (TQE).

This book provides the basic tools administrators and teachers need to bring the processes and systems in their schools under statistical control. The reader should note that neither of the terms *reducing variance* nor *statistical control* is intended to imply reducing people into numbers or reducing education to robotics. Enhancing quality in education is the heart of the matter. Proper use of these tools, as expertly illustrated by Professors Latta and Downey, will aid readers in their quest to provide their students with a Total Quality Education.

Larry E. Frase
San Diego State University

✧ ✧

Preface

Some will argue that education has changed very little over time. Problems that existed 20 years ago are still with us today and are likely to be with us into the early years of the 21st century. Likely, that is, unless educators can become more skilled at problem solving.

In this book, we demonstrate that a wide array of sophisticated tools for problem solving are currently available. They are *quality tools*, which we have adapted for use within groups. Because education is a people business, we take care to ensure that the tools selected for inclusion in this book do not dehumanize or distance people from the problem-solving process. In addition, these quality tools include parents and students in the groups as much as possible. Too often we educators become blinded in our efforts to deliver the curriculum and miss giving the learner the information, skills, and tools he or she needs to assume a greater responsibility for his or her own learning. Teachers and assistant principals are forever dealing with situations resulting from students' inability to solve their own problems. For this reason, we advocate teaching students the quality tools, which may very well result in the greatest value-added component of Total Quality Education.

Chapter 1 develops the rationale for educational stakeholders to consider quality tools. Variance in quality exists everywhere. When a situation is of value to us, tools are used to measure and monitor the reduction of variance. Because no system is perfect, it is impossible to reduce variance to zero, but it *can* be reduced. If education is truly valued, why not identify and monitor the reduction of variance in education? Why has the drop-out situation been with us so long? Why is the perceived solution to most problems in education "more money"? Most educational problems could be eliminated through cross-functional groups of educators armed with powerful quality tools that are properly applied. However, improper use of these tools by a group of uncommitted individuals leaves educational problem-solvers dealing only with superficial symptoms rather than with real problems.

Chapter 2 highlights three quality group process tools—brainstorming, the nominal group technique, and the focus group. Educators have used the first two tools in homogeneous groups, but more often than not these problem-solving efforts have resulted in solutions that have created more problems. By contrast, the third tool introduces the selection of groups from across the various functions of educational systems whose members bring new thinking into the group think tank. Parents, students, and representatives from business add even richer thinking into this problem-solving process. The focus group promises to be a valuable tool for educators especially when members are armed with knowledge of how, where, when, and why to use the powerful quality tools discussed in Chapters 3, 4, and 5.

In Chapter 3 we discuss the seven basic quality tools, often referred to as statistical process control (SPC) quality tools—histograms, pareto charts, scatter diagrams, run charts, control charts, cause-and-effect diagrams, and flowcharts. An eighth quality tool, check sheets, is so familiar to educators that we did not include it in this text. Numerous uses of these tools are suggested for each of four levels within the educational system—district, school, classroom, and student/home. We intend that all the quality tools be used within cross-functional groups. Parents and students should be included as group members whenever practical so they can learn through participation in real-life problem solving.

Chapter 4 introduces seven additional quality tools that move cross-functional groups into the beginning stages of planning and management—affinity diagrams, tree diagrams, matrices, interrelationship digraphs, radar diagrams, force-field analysis, and benchmarking. Planning and subsequently managing the implementation of solution strategies become of utmost importance once real problems—not just symptoms—have been identified.

Action planning and activity networks, presented in Chapter 5, are integrative quality tools familiar to some educators. Some may also have heard of the Plan-Do-Check-Act (PDCA) cycle, but few have any knowledge of Hoshin planning. The breakthrough concept nested within the philosophy and practice of Hoshin planning is the single most powerful tool presented in this text.

Where and how should the systemic use of quality tools begin? We present more tools in this book than perhaps any one individual might use. Within cross-functional groups, however, the collective group may well already have expertise in all of these tools. We envision both individuals and groups consistently using quality tools throughout all levels of the school system. It is not important who begins the learning process that leads to this practice; it is only important that we begin. Chapter 6 lights the torch and passes it to you, the reader. Because quality tools must be utilized within a total systems approach to Continuous Quality Improvement (CQI), we strongly suggest that some of the references that follow the Preface be read concurrently with this text to give an understanding of the broader framework for using quality tools.

Raymond F. Latta
Carolyn J. Downey
San Diego State University

References

Argyris, C. (1988). *Reasoning, learning, and action*. San Francisco: Jossey-Bass.

Argyris, C. (1990). *Overcoming organizational defenses*. New York: Prentice-Hall.

Barth, R. S. (1991). *Improving schools from within.* San Francisco: Jossey-Bass.

Bechtell. M. L. (1993). *Untangling organizational gridlock: Strategies for building a customer focus.* Milwaukee, WI: ASQC Quality Press.

Bonstingl, J. J. (1991). *Schools of quality: An introduction to total quality management in education.* Alexandria, VA: Association for Supervision and Curriculum Development.

Byrnes, M. A., Cornesky, R. A., & Byrnes, L. W. (1992). *The quality teacher: Implementing total quality in the classroom.* Bunnell, FL: Cornesky & Associates.

Cartin, T. J. (1993). *Principles & practices of TQM.* Milwaukee, WI: ASQC Quality Press.

Crosby, P. B. (1984). *Quality without tears.* New York: McGraw-Hill.

Fiske, E. B. (1991). *Smart schools: Smart kids.* New York: Simon & Schuster.

Glasser, W. (1990). *The quality school.* New York: Harper & Row.

Johnson, R. S. (1993). *TQM management processes for quality operations.* Milwaukee, WI: ASQC Quality Press.

Miller, G. L., & Krumm, L. L. (1992). *The whats, whys, and hows of quality improvement.* Milwaukee, WI: ASQC Quality Press.

Rinehart, G. (1992). *Quality education.* Milwaukee, WI: ASQC Quality Press.

Schenkat, R. (1993). *Quality connections: Transforming schools through total quality management.* Alexandria, VA: Association for Supervision and Curriculum Development.

3 M Corporation. (1992). *Managing quality education: The process for improvement.* St. Paul: Author.

✧   ✧

About the Authors

Raymond F. Latta is Professor of Educational Leadership at San Diego State University, where he directs the Center for Educational Management (CEMRT) and an International Graduate Program in Educational Leadership, one of two graduate programs offered by CEMRT. He completed his Ph.D. in educational systems and planning at Florida State University. He has 21 years of experience in higher education, including 7 years as a Department of Educational Administration chair. In addition, he taught in public schools for 3 years in British Columbia, Canada, and was principal for 1 year of a K-12 school system in Oakville, Washington.

Born in British Columbia, Latta has been an international consultant for 22 years. His areas of expertise include strategic planning, quality leadership, guiding district and school efforts in utilizing quality indicators, and establishing benchmarks (educational standards). He has published more than 100 articles, handbooks, and manuals. He most recently coauthored 4 manuals: *A Systemic Approach to Planning: Leading Education in British Columbia Into the 21st Century; Preparing for the Future: Making Strategic Thinking, Strategic leadership, and Renewal Part of Everyday Life Into the 21st Century; Conduction Opinion Surveys: Gathering Data and Input From Educational Stakeholders;* and *Developing Indicators and Standards: Choosing Appropriate Measures and Targets of Educational Performance,* all published by the British Columbia Superintendents' Association, Vancouver, B.C.

Carolyn J. Downey is an Associate Professor of Educational Leadership at San Diego State University. She has 22 years of experience in school administration, including 10 years as an assistant superintendent in two school systems and 4 years as superintendent of the Kyrene School district in Tempe, Arizona. She served as an associate in an educational research and development organization for 4 years and left education for 1 year to serve as a health care research consultant. Her expertise includes quality leadership, organizational development, human resource development, curriculum and instruction, and program evaluation. She completed her M.A. in educational psychology at the University of Southern California and her Ph.D. at Arizona State University. She has published numerous articles and has written several chapters in books, including *Motivating and Compensating Teachers* (1992). She has been an international consultant for over 2 decades, presenting and speaking in hundreds of school systems as well as state and national organizations. In 1975 she was recognized as a National Academy for School Executives Distinguished Professor by the American Association of School Administrators.

❖ 1 ❖

Using Quality Tools in School Systems

There was a dachshund once, so long
He hadn't any notion
How long it took to notify
His tail of his emotion;
And so it happened, while his eyes
were filled with woe and sadness,
His little tail went wagging on
Because of previous gladness.

JOHN F. KENNEDY

We find education in a situation where many professional educators, like the dachshund in the poem, may be smiling because of previous successes. The general public, however, has been dissatisified with our educational system for the last decade, first asking for minor reform and more recently calling for major restructuring. What is the correct perception of the status of our present educational system? Do we have sufficient quantitative and qualitative data to guide us in making changes? The answer to these two questions is that we simply do not know. To clear up this situation, we need indicators, some baseline data to use as benchmarks so that progress can be measured and improvements can be made. We need quality tools for ensuring quality now and into the 21st century.

Determining Why, How, and Where
Quality Tools Fit Into Total Quality Education

Most professions have tools of the trade. A few professions may not have a set of definable tools and, indeed, may not have a need for them. Education, however, is unique in the following: (a) It is one of the oldest professions; (b) it is one of the biggest businesses in the world, becoming more so every year in terms of both size and cost; (c) it does not have a set of unanimously accepted tools of its trade; and (d) everyone claims, having completed anywhere from 6 to 20 years of education, to be an expert regarding its practice. Clearly, the education profession would benefit from precise tools as well as from people with expertise in using these tools.

In order to successfully add to the toolbox of their profession, educators need to

- Think "adapt" rather than "adopt"
- Understand that tools add leverage, strengthening or extending one's ability to work more effectively and efficiently
- Realize that it is the human factor that makes tools effective or ineffective
- Realize that an opportunity overlooked may be an opportunity missed
- Model lifelong learning of tools that hold promise to education, accepting that how and where to use these tools is the responsibility of everyone within the profession

Given these five-fold keys, educators will be able to explore the potential of quality tools before the educational system irreparably breaks down. Consistent with the tenets of Total Quality Education (TQE), the quality tools discussed within this book provide the foundation for Continuous Quality Improvement (CQI). Educational systems in many countries have already embarked on district- and school-based improvement, as evidenced by their strategic planning efforts and by annual reports to educational stakeholders. Accountability has arrived (Figure 1.1).

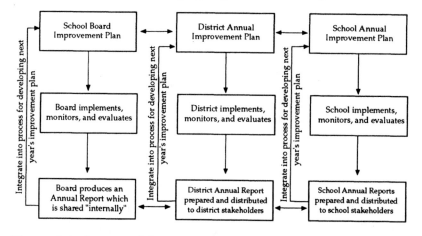

Figure 1.1. Accountability as a System

The main differences between TQE and other educational improvement efforts to date are the following:

1. TQE means total, everyone, all systems.
2. TQE focuses on quality as seen mainly, but not solely, through the customer's eyes.
3. TQE offers a set of tools that promise to assist us in our quest and journey towards CQI.

Tools that both increase our effectiveness as educators and assist us in responding with professional accountability are welcomed; tools that do otherwise have no place in our profession. It is a mistake, however, to think that the use of quality tools guarantees quality. Although the tools provide more and better information, just using them does not ensure a high-quality school system. Instead, quality tools exist to extend individual effectiveness, help solve problems, gather information and analyze data, and assist in making decisions about processes and systems.

Even at its best, change in education is slow. Lacking sophisticated tools, educators have tended to lose momentum, reacting to perceptions unsubstantiated by accurate information and/or responding to symptoms of a problem instead of the real problem. Educational or not, problems are much like icebergs—the major portion remains hidden below the surface (Figure 1.2).

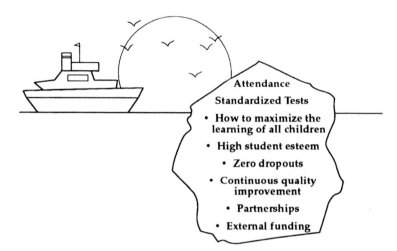

Figure 1.2. Educational Quality Indicators, Problems, and Solutions are Like Icebergs: 10% Visible, 90% Invisible

By using proper tools for problem identification and analysis, educators might well discover that most problems are not only solvable but are also better met as challenges. Quality tools therefore promise to equip committed educators to more easily visualize and meet their challenges.

Reducing Variance: Why Quality Tools Are Needed

Have you ever noticed how many people are careful with money that is theirs but wasteful of money that is not? Perhaps you have heard how a hammer worth about four dollars ended up costing hundreds of dollars when purchased through the military bureaucracy. And ashtrays have ended up costing even more. These horror stories depict variance at an extreme. The following are general beliefs of what happens when public services become large bureaucracies:

- Waste is the rule rather than the exception.
- No one is concerned about performance, productivity, or accountability.

- The golden rule is "penny-wise and pound-foolish."
- Change is impossible.
- Costs are not only beyond the public's control, but also "the more you pay, the less you get."
- Extreme variances are expected and accepted.

Educators know that there is only a little truth in all of the above opinions when applied to education. What we need is a process for communicating our countless successes and significant achievements to the public. This process must leave no doubt that education is still the best investment in any country's future. To accomplish this, tools that both measure quality and are acceptable to the general public are required. These are the quality tools that this book intends to place in the educator's toolbox.

Although quality tools can help to display data, sharpen communication, and change public perceptions about education as a profession, their greatest value lies in identifying and monitoring the reduction of variance. The public would like us to ensure that they are getting the most for each public school dollar spent; in other words, to treat their money as though it were our own. Likewise, they would also like us to treat educational systems the way we treat other systems we value. For example, think of things outside of education that we do preventive maintenance on *before* they break: the roofs on our houses, our relationships, our bank accounts, our cars, our health, and so on. You may ask what variance has to do with this. The answer is, Everything!

Variance results from two basic causes—the common and the special. Common causes (lack of feedback, unclear priorities, insufficient training, overextended or outdated procedures) create fairly small random variances, which can be monitored and reduced using quality tools but which rarely call for a major system overhall. On the other hand, special causes of variance (faulty procedures, failure to follow procedures, inaccurate input, or reluctance to change) create variances well beyond what is considered expected or acceptable. Such wide variances almost always result in major overhauls or changes. When systems are kept under control, the small common causes of variance can continuously be reduced, and when systems are continuously improved, quality is continuously improved. The result is Continuous Quality Improvement. Using quality tools with out-of-control systems is of little value, except to validate that a system is, indeed, out of control.

Variance and tools for identifying and reducing it are commonplace. Variance is everywhere, even in the air we breathe. Very little remains the same from one moment to the next. We measure the variability of things that are important or valuable to us with tools that have been tested and determined to be accurate. Consider, for example, Table 1.1.

TABLE 1.1. Tools for Measuring Variance in Systems of Real Value to Us

Systems of Values	Tools for Measuring Variance
Overall circulatory system of the human body	Thermometer
Human heart as a system	Pulse rate Blood pressure
Car engine	Oil pressure gauge Engine temperature gauge
Educational system	Standardized tests QUALITY TOOLS

We know that the average body temperature is 98.6°F. However, because we also know that our temperature is not always the same, we allow an acceptable variance. In short, we set an upper and lower limit, accepting as within normal range a body temperature of ± 1.5°F. Although there may be reason for concern if our temperature rises above or falls below this range, we do not panic. We simply seek the cause or an explanation for this unacceptable variance. You may think of tools that you have devised to measure the variability of things or situations you value, thus maintaining an acceptable range of variance. No one will argue the real value of education, but look at our lack of tools. A standardized test may not be a very good tool, but it is one of the few that exists. We have attempted to improve standardized tests as quality indicators, but not much has changed. In fact, the inappropriateness of this tool is exhibited by the continued high variability in drop-out rates between districts, states, provinces, and countries. Are we simply unaware of the right tools for measuring CQI in education?

We can examine CQI further by comparing the way marksmen improve their accuracy and effectiveness with the ways traditional educational systems have attempted to improve their effectiveness. In Figure 1.3, both the marksman and education are illustrated as out of control during the first stage. The second stage illustrates that some focusing has taken place. With practice, the marksman continues to reduce the variance and move the grouping of shots closer to the bull's eye, illustrating Continuous Quality Improvement. Education, on the other hand, appears willing to consider *any* change as evidence of improvement, even when there may be an unacceptable rate of variance. For example, a few things hit the bull's eye in the figure, but the dropout rate remains 30% (no evidence of Continuous Quality Improvement).

Why do so many people succeed in continuously improving their marksmanship using a tool as simple as a target? The secret just may be the right tool, a lot of practice, and a commitment to Continuous Quality Improvement! We need a spirit, a commitment, and a philosophy at least equal to this to cascade throughout all of our educational systems.

Educators who value education should have a rather extensive toolbox. However, when we looked we found that toolbox almost bare: Standardized tests and a folder labeled "alternative assessment" were there, and not much more. Even though some educational targets or standards exist, some appear to be of doubtful value, as Figure 1.3 illustrates. The few tools found in the alternative assessment folder are weak and probably are not acceptable to the public at large. In contrast, most of the quality tools in this book can assist educators in measuring and reducing variance in educational systems.

A final thought for those not yet convinced that tools are of any real value to committed educators. If you believe education in

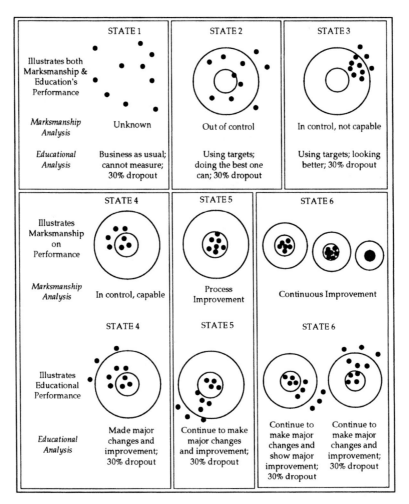

Figure 1.3. Equating Traditional Educational Improvement Efforts With Improving Your Marksmanship

your school district, school, or classroom is already on the right road to improvement, think about the thousands of drivers who are on the right road and driving between the white lines but who are killed through no fault of their own. Even our road system is subject to unacceptable variance. Will Rogers had a saying that perhaps best summarizes this concept: "Even if you're on the right track, you'll get run over if you just sit there." Being "on the right track" is at best only part of what it takes for a journey of Continuous Quality Improvement.

Introducing the Quality Tools

The quality tools in this text are discussed throughout Chapters 2, 3, 4 and 5 in the sequence in which they appear in Figure 1.4. The first three tools exemplify the points we continually emphasize about using all quality tools within groups, preferably cross-functional groups. Two heads are always better than one, and three or more are better than two. In addition, by working in groups, the quality tools help to

- Engage the participation of those who "own" a problem in the problem-solving process
- Create ownership in solution strategies that evolve out of the group process
- Dispel the saying that "sometimes liars figure and figures lie," because the figures and data are supplied by group members
- Change suspicions that shroud the use of data and quantitative analysis to confidence in using applications that are appropriate and add value
- Demonstrate how educators may adapt a tool or process to make it work specifically in educational settings
- Create a learning situation where each member of the group learns why, where, when, and how to use quality tools
- Humanize the use of quality tools by educators
- Ensure that we recognize the real value is always *people* and not the tool or tools; that is, tools in and of themselves accomplish nothing but are merely implements that, when guided by human intellect, can increase human potential, productivity, effectiveness, and efficiency

Quality Improvement Tools and Techniques		Problem Solving Process					
		Problem Identification	Problem Analysis	Establish Objectives	Examine Solution Strategies	Implement Action Plans	Evaluate and Revise Based on Feedback
Group Process	Brainstorming	X	X		X		
	Nominal Group Process	X	X		X		
	Focus Group	X	X		X		X
Basic Quality Tools	Histograms	X	X				X
	Pareto Charts	X	X				X
	Scatter Diagrams	X	X				X
	Run Charts	X	X				X
	Control Charts	X	X				X
	Cause & Effect Diagrams	X	X		X		X
	Flowcharts	X	X		X	X	X
Prelude to Planning and Management	Affinity Diagrams		X			X	
	Tree Diagrams		X			X	
	Matrices Diagrams				X	X	
	Interrelationship		X	X	X		
	Radar Diagrams	X	X	X			X
	Force-Field Analysis	X	X	X	X		
	Benchmarking	X	X	X	X		X
Integrative Quality Tools	Action Planning	X	X	X	X	X	X
	Activity Networks	X	X	X	X	X	X
	Plan-Do-Check-Act Cycle	X	X	X	X	X	X
	Hoshin Planning	X	X	X	X	X	X

Figure 1.4. Quality Tools: Their Use and Relativity to the Problem-Solving Process

Group process tools or techniques provide the value-added component necessary for the quality tools to be of substantive use in education.

Summary

People outside of education (politicians, parents, the business community, taxpayers) almost all agree that education is in need of major restructuring. Educators, on the other hand, often appear to be content to continue with business as usual. In both the business and the public sectors, organizations are choosing to pursue quality. We recommend that educators also learn all they can about quality philosophy, principles, concepts, theories, tools, and practices. Determine what is worthy of adapting, do some field testing, and take new steps in the direction of quality.

Key Terms and Concepts

Accountability. This is the process of accepting, implementing, monitoring, completing, and reporting progress made toward meeting responsibilities in both a timely and an accurately communicated manner.

Adapt. This refers to adjusting to better fit a particular situation. The quality tools discussed in this text have been adapted for use within group processes in education.

Adopt. Business and education are not similar enough to adopt each other's successes without careful examination, pilot testing, and considerable adaptations.

Continuous Quality Improvement (CQI). Because quality is a moving target, one must always seek to improve one's products and systems by continuously reducing variance. Such a process is referred to as CQI.

Group use of quality tools. The best way to resolve problems is to be a part of the problem-identification, -analysis, and -solving process. When people are grouped, armed with quality tools, and have access to data and information, they learn to solve their problems together. Within such a process, everyone's problem-solving skills continuously improve over time.

Quality. This term refers to the type of philosophy, process, and practice involved in meeting and exceeding the needs of one's customers/learners.

Quality tools. This refers to hardware, software, processes, models, and techniques that measure and monitor system improvements, assist educators in reducing variance, and thus meet and exceed the needs of customers/learners.

Reducing variance. Normal variance between upper and lower limits can be monitored and reduced by continuously improving the responsible system. When variance exceeds these limits (i.e., is uncontrolled and unexpected), an entirely new system or process may be needed.

Superficial problem solving. Without careful analysis using specific tools, symptoms of problems are tackled without coming to a resolution. When quality is desired, problem identification and analysis are obtained using quality tools to bypass the symptoms and get to the root of the problem.

Tool. An implement, process, model, or technique that extends human capability.

Value-added. One way to get a job done is simply to act the way others before you have, that is, "doing things right." Another way is to examine, based on your experience, how things might be done better than in the past and, using critical and strategic thinking, add your value to the effort. Doing the "right" thing more adds value and results in Continuous Quality Improvement.

Variance. This term refers to deviations in process. No matter how perfect a process or a system is, there will always be slight deviations from the ideal.

References and Sources for Additional Reading

Deming, W. E. (1982). *Out of the crisis.* Cambridge: MIT Press.
Gavin, D. A. (1988). *Managing quality: The strategic and competitive edge.* New York: Free Press.
Gitlow, H. S., & Gitlow, S. T. (1987). *The Deming guide to quality and competitive position.* Englewood Cliffs, NJ: Prentice-Hall.
Hammer, M. (1990, July-August). Reengineering work: Don't automate, obliterate. *Harvard Business Review,* pp. 104-112.
Joiner, B. L., & Gaudard, M. A. (1990, December). Variation, management and W. E. Deming. *Quality Progess,* pp. 29-30.
Litchfield, R. (1991, February). Solving an educational crisis: Business has finally tired of an education system that produces

illiterates and of its own shoddy record of training employees. *Canadian Business*, pp. 29-30.

McManus, D. R. (1992, October). Creating Canada's future. *Quality Progress*, pp. 29-30.

Miller, L. M., & Howard, J. (1990). *Managing quality through TEAMS: A workbook for team leaders & members.* Atlanta, GA: The Miller Company.

Nolan, T. W., & Provost, L. P. (1990, May). Understanding variation. *Quality Progress*, pp. 70-71.

✦ 2 ✦

Using Quality Group Process Tools

If we don't change our direction, we might end up where we're headed.

CHINESE PROVERB

The majority of people who choose education as a profession have greater sensitivity toward people and their development than they do toward the use of tools to simply get a gob done as quickly and as inexpensively as possible. Education is also big business, but it differs in the minds of most educators from business in the private sector. Educators fear that successful solutions from the private sector will inappropriately be adopted in education simply to force change or reduce costs. There is also a fear that business tools will dehumanize processes, coming between educators and their primary customers (learners).

Because using quality group process tools can help allay the above concerns of educators, they are presented prior to the more technical or precise quality tools. All of the quality tools are suitable, even preferable, for use in groups, although individuals may use the more technical tools apart from a group. The techniques and tools can be adapted to each group situation and used in whatever way group members feel most comfortable.

The quality group process tools described in this chapter are brainstorming, nominal group technique, and focus groups. They emphasize involvement and are consistent with the saying, *"Tell me, I forget; show me, I remember; involve me, I understand."*

Brainstorming Strategies

Understanding the What, Why,
and How of Brainstorming Strategies

SCENARIO: At a district community advisory meeting, the few people in attendance are asked to identify the major challenges or problems facing their district. They brainstorm and generate a list of challenges (see Figure 2.1).

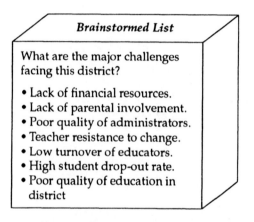

Brainstormed List

What are the major challenges facing this district?

• Lack of financial resources.
• Lack of parental involvement.
• Poor quality of administrators.
• Teacher resistance to change.
• Low turnover of educators.
• High student drop-out rate.
• Poor quality of education in district

Figure 2.1. List of Major Challenges Facing the District

What Is It?

Brainstorming is an idea-generation technique. It allows you to generate a list of ideas through group participation in a risk-free environment.

Why Use It?

This technique helps to generate ideas for improvement projects, identify possible causes of problems, and list ways of addressing an issue, just to name a few applications. It stimulates creativity, encourages group participation, and minimizes premature critiquing and evaluation of ideas.

How Do You Create It?

The following steps are used in brainstorming:

1. State the topic. Clearly write and underline the topic at the top of a flip chart or board.
2. Establish a time limit for the process.
3. Explain the rules of brainstorming to participants. Ask questions. Obtain agreement/consensus. The following are the rules:
   - Everyone is encouraged to participate and to be creative.
   - All ideas are good; evaluating/critiquing/criticizing of ideas is not allowed.
   - A large number of ideas should be generated.
   - Participants are allowed to "piggy-back" off each other's ideas.
   - All ideas presented are recorded.
   - Participants may offer more than one idea at a time.
4. Record all ideas in a text large enough for everyone to see.
5. After all ideas have been generated, clarify ideas as needed.
6. Organize the ideas into categories, identify additional categories to include, and add within each category.

Educational Uses of Brainstorming

Figure 2.2 suggests uses and examples of brainstorming at various levels within education. Brainstorming is a free-flowing process that can be done by almost any size group. The examples provided are hypothetical and can also involve both students and their parents. Adults are often unable to express their creativity, but our youth have fewer boundaries and will use quality tools like

Level	Potential Areas of Use	Sample Use
District	• Identify challenges or problems facing school district. • List suggestions for downsizing school district. • Identify strategies for raising money for district. • Identify suggestions for increasing parent involvement district-wide. • List strategies for improving the quality of education in the district.	**BRAINSTORMED LIST** What are some of the strategies for improving the quality of education in our district? • Form partnerships with business. • Utilize technology better. • Hire a quality expert. • Train parents, teachers and administrators in continuous quality improvement. • Require newly hired educators in the district to also be entrepreneurs. • Reduce dropout rate.
School	• Identify challenges facing the school. • Develop a list of reasons of why students drop out of this school. • Develop a list of strategies for increasing engaged academic learning time in the school. • Develop a list of suggestions for supervising students during recess. • Identify suggestions for reducing discipline problems in the school. • Identify strategies for improving the quality of education in the school.	**BRAINSTORMED LIST** How can we improve the quality of education in this school? • Get a new principal. • Keep and support our principal. • Give all certified, classified students and parents training in Continuous Quality Improvement. • Create a situation of 100% attendance. • Quit fighting among ourselves. • Secure additional support through business partnership. • Become a customer driven school.
Classroom Teacher	• Generate ideas from students and parents in how to become a customer-based classroom. • Identify a list of suggestions from students on how to reduce the need for discipline. • Identify a list of suggestions on how to get homework and assignments in on time. • Identify strategies for raising the class average on the utilized standardized test by at least 5%.	**BRAINSTORMED LIST** What are the factors critical to developing a customer-based classroom? • Care about students as people and learners. • Like students. • Listen to students and parents. • Teacher, students and parents have access to continuous quality improvement training. • Students assume a greater responsibility for their own learning. • Set up some aspects of class to model an enterprise system.
Students (within school and/or home)	• Develop a list of desirable jobs with good pay. • List people in the community who the students both believe in and who they would like to have as class speakers. • List ways in which they can help and support each other. • List reasons why attendance is important. • List ways of improving student-parent relationship.	**BRAINSTORMED LIST** What are the ways of improving student-parent relationship? • Parents listen to child. • Child listens to parent. • Parent is home when needed. • Child follows simple (few) rules. • Parent sets few simple rules. • Parent and child celebrate their successes together.

Figure 2.2. Educational Uses of Brainstorming at Various Levels

brainstorming to push their problem-solving efforts to the limit. Many of these contributions, beyond our adult limits and outside of our thought patterns, are valuable to the process of Continuous Quality Improvement.

Nominal Group Technique

Understanding the What, Why, and How of the Nominal Group Technique

SCENARIO: Members at a district community advisory meeting are asked to identify and prioritize the challenges facing the school district. They brainstorm and prioritize the identified challenges using the nominal group technique (NGT) (Figure 2.3).

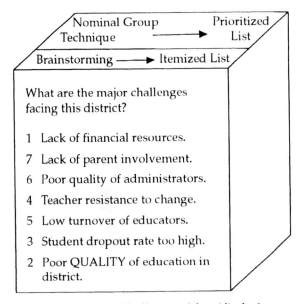

Figure 2.3. List of District Challenges Identified via Brainstorming and Prioritized via NGT

What Is It?

The *nominal group technique* (NGT) is a formalized form of brainstorming developed by Andre Delbecq and Andrew Van de Ven in the late 1960s at the University of Wisconsin. It consists of generating responses to a predetermined question. The final ranking combines the judgments of group members in order to reach a group decision or consensus.

Why Use It?

This technique helps to generate, narrow down, and focus ideas for improvement projects or for solving problems. It can also be used to identify and consolidate issues that need to be addressed.

How Do You Create It?

The following steps are used in the NGT:

1. State the task or problem. Write this statement on flip chart paper and post in a prominent location. Ensure that the statement is unambiguous and understood by all.
2. Allow participants 5 to 15 minutes of silence to individually write responses to the task problem statement.
3. Each member states one response (or passes, at his or her option); no discussion should occur. Record all responses on a flip chart.
4. When all suggestions have been listed, clarify them without evaluation. Duplicate items are eliminated only if the originator of the idea agrees.
5. Having clarified and eliminated duplication, individuals prioritize the suggestions. The following "card-sorting" technique, although not critical to this process, reduces the list to a manageable size.

Card-sort to reduce a large list to nine (9) items:

a. Number the items in the large list from 1 to 50 (or what-ever the upper limit happens to be). The items may be numbered at random or however you choose (Figure 2.4).

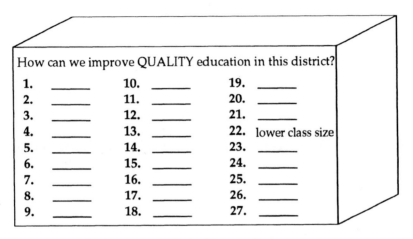

How can we improve QUALITY education in this district?

1. _____	10. _____	19. _____
2. _____	11. _____	20. _____
3. _____	12. _____	21. _____
4. _____	13. _____	22. lower class size
5. _____	14. _____	23. _____
6. _____	15. _____	24. _____
7. _____	16. _____	25. _____
8. _____	17. _____	26. _____
9. _____	18. _____	27. _____

Figure 2.4. Brainstormed List of Suggestions

b. Give each individual a set of 3″ by 5″ cards using the following as a guide:
   –10-20 items, give four cards
   –21-35 items, give six cards (see Figure 2.5)
   –36-50 items, give eight cards

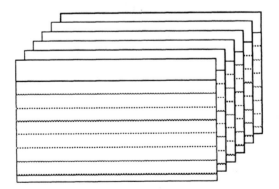

Figure 2.5. Six 3″ × 5″ Cards Given to Participants

c. Instruct each individual to select the six most important suggestions from the large list and to write one suggestion along with its corresponding number in the center of each 3" by 5" card (Figure 2.6).

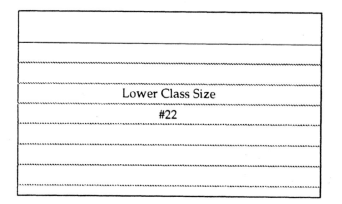

Figure 2.6. Card Format

Note: Let us suppose that #22 on the long list of suggestions is "lower class size" and that it is one of the six most important suggestions to you on the list. You simply write the suggestion in the center of one of your 3" by 5" cards and place the #22 under it.

d. Follow the process outlined in "c" until you have placed each of your six most important suggestions in the center of a 3" by 5" card along with its corresponding number.

e. Considering now only the six items you selected and placed on the 3" by 5" cards, place your six cards in order of priority, with the most important first and the least important last (Figure 2.7).

f. Assign weighting points to each of your six 3" by 5" cards; place the number of points assigned to each suggestion in the upper right-hand corner of each card; give six points to your most important suggestion and one point to the least important (Figure 2.8).

g. The cards are then collected and sorted using the number in the center of each 3" by 5" card (Figure 2.8).

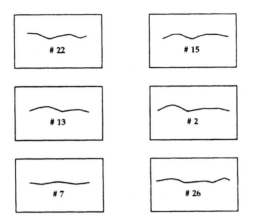

Figure 2.7. Setup of Six Cards

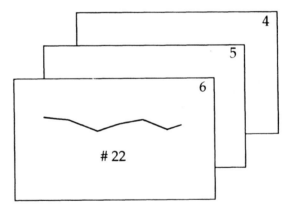

Figure 2.8. Ranking of Cards in Upper Right-Hand Corner

    h. Once the cards are sorted, the points in each upper right-hand corner are tallied for each stack of cards (Figure 2.9).
    i. The total points for each stack of cards is then placed alongside each corresponding suggestion on the large composite list (Figure 2.9).
    j. Make up a new list of suggestions containing the nine suggestions receiving the most points.
  6. Discuss and clarify the nine surviving suggestions until everyone is comfortable with the list.

How can we improve QUALITY education in this district?			
6 points	1	16 points	8
19 points	2	etc. . .	9
22 points	3	etc. . .	10
13 points	4	etc. . .	11
27 points	5		12
81 points	6		13
31 points	7		14

Figure 2.9. Illustration of Tallying

7. Prioritize the remaining nine suggestions (Figure 2.10). The previous exercise has narrowed the large list into nine suggestions of equal significance. The next "card-sort" will give everyone an opportunity to rank the importance of all nine suggestions using the process outlined in Figure 2.10.

Educational Uses of the Nominal Group Technique (NGT)

Figure 2.11 illustrates uses of the nominal group technique. Examples from the previous discussion on the brainstorming process are used to show how these two quality tools may be integrated.

Focus Groups/Teams

Understanding the What, Why, and How of Focus Groups/Teams

SCENARIO: At a recent meeting, the district community advisory committee followed a process that identified the lack of financial resources as a major problem. A focus group made up of

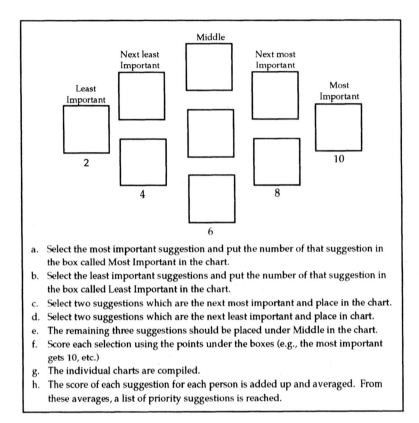

a. Select the most important suggestion and put the number of that suggestion in the box called Most Important in the chart.
b. Select the least important suggestions and put the number of that suggestion in the box called Least Important in the chart.
c. Select two suggestions which are the next most important and place in the chart.
d. Select two suggestions which are the next least important and place in chart.
e. The remaining three suggestions should be placed under Middle in the chart.
f. Score each selection using the points under the boxes (e.g., the most important gets 10, etc.)
g. The individual charts are compiled.
h. The score of each suggestion for each person is added up and averaged. From these averages, a list of priority suggestions is reached.

Figure 2.10. Suggested Ranking Process

two people from the committee, along with eight others from throughout the district, was established to research this issue. The group's mission was to gather further data and to ensure that a real problem, rather than just a symptom of a problem, had been identified. The group studied the roles and responsibilities of "focus groups" and unanimously agreed to utilize the process illustrated in Figure 2.12.

What Is It?

A *focus group* or team is a group of people selected from across educational stakeholder groups that is charged with focusing on

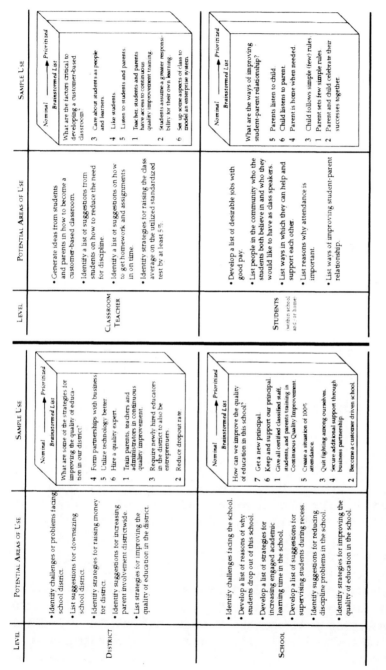

LEVEL	POTENTIAL AREAS OF USE	SAMPLE USE
DISTRICT	• Identify challenges or problems facing school district. • List suggestions for downsizing school district. • Identify strategies for raising money for district. • Identify suggestions for increasing parent involvement districtwide. • List strategies for improving the quality of education in the district.	Nominal → Prioritized *Brainstormed List* What are some of the strategies for improving the quality of education in our district? 4 Form partnerships with business. 5 Utilize technology better. 6 Hire a quality expert. 1 Train parents, teachers and administrators in continuous quality improvement. 3 Require newly hired educators in the district to also be entreprenuers. 2 Reduce dropout rate.
SCHOOL	• Identify challenges facing the school. • Develop a list of reasons of why students drop out of this school. • Develop a list of strategies for increasing engaged academic learning time in the school. • Develop a list of suggestions for supervising students during recess. • Identify suggestions for reducing discipline problems in the school. • Identify strategies for improving the quality of education in the school.	Nominal → Prioritized *Brainstormed List* How can we improve the quality of education in this school? 7 Get a new principal. 6 Keep and support our principal. 1 Give all certified classified staff, students, and parents training in Continuous Quality Improvement. 5 Create a situation of 100% attendance. 3 Quit fighting among ourselves. 4 Secure additional support through business partnership. 2 Become a customer driven school.
CLASSROOM TEACHER	• Generate ideas from students and parents in how to become a customer-based classroom. • Identify a list of suggestions from students on how to reduce the need for discipline. • Identify a list of suggestions on how to get homework and assignments in on time. • Identify strategies for raising the class average on the utilized standardized test by at least 5%.	Nominal → Prioritized *Brainstormed List* What are the factors critical to developing a customer-based classroom? 3 Care about students as people and learners. 4 Like students. 5 Listen to students and parents. 1 Teacher, students and parents have access to continuous quality improvement training. 2 Students assume a greater responsibility for their own learning. 6 Set up some aspects of class to model an enterprise system.
STUDENTS within school and/or home	• Develop a list of desirable jobs with good pay. • List people in the community who the students both believe in and who they would like to have as class speakers. • List ways in which they can help and support each other. • List reasons why attendance is important. • List ways of improving student-parent relationship.	Nominal → Prioritized *Brainstormed List* What are the ways of improving student-parent relationship? 5 Parents listen to child. 6 Child listens to parent. 4 Parent is home when needed. 3 Child follows simple (few) rules. 1 Parent sets few simple rules. 2 Parent and child celebrate their successes together.

Figure 2.11. Educational Uses of NGT at Various Levels

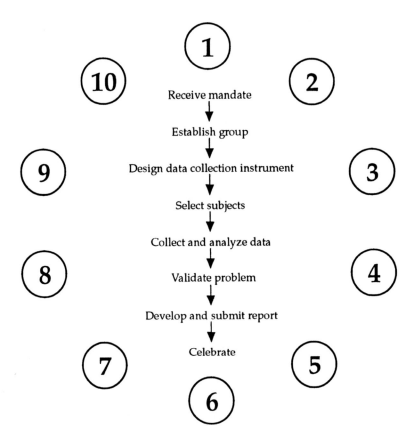

Figure 2.12. Focus Group Process

a specific problem. Its task is usually to conduct more research to validate the problem, to recommend an improvement objective, and/or to suggest criteria for selecting a solution strategy.

Why Use It?

Too often groups attempt to solve so many problems that they end up solving nothing. Focus groups are used to determine whether the problems under consideration have been identified as real and validated across educational stakeholder groups. A cross-functional group or team is usually best because expertise outside of the situation under study is often necessary to ensure that the group's analysis and recommendations do not result in simply *more of the same.*

How Do You Create It?

The following steps are used to establish and utilize focus groups or teams as a quality tool (review Figure 2.12):

1. Identify a problem within the educational system appropriate for the focus group process and develop a mandate for using this process. Regardless of the problem or challenge, it is usually qualitative in nature and will require a great deal of further clarification.
2. Establish a time frame and criteria for selecting a moderator.
   - The time frame is usually 3 to 6 months.
   - The ideal group moderator or facilitator is
     –Not gender- or ethnically-biased
     –Flexible
     –Admits biases relative to the problem
     –Insightful about people, and a good listener with a sense of humor
     –Not defensive
     –Empowering
3. Select eight to twelve members per group across functional lines within the district and seek to include, where appropriate, parents, community members, and students. Resist the tendency to make groups larger or homogeneous.
4. Have the focus group come together, and give members the following:
   - In-service training on quality tools they might find beneficial (e.g., brainstorming, NGT, flowchart, action plans)
   - An opportunity to get acquainted
   - A detailed outline of their mission, the time frame, the available resources, etc.
   - A promise to celebrate together when the challenge has been met

5. Have the group identify information needs, establish data collection strategies (e.g., interviews, questionnaires, personal testimony), and develop research questions.
6. Next, have members pilot test possible data-collection instruments.
7. Select participants, randomly or otherwise, who will be involved in the study/research.
8. Gather and analyze the data.
9. Validate or substantiate the problem and support the group's findings and recommendations with factual data and/or testimonials.
10. Draft and submit a report documenting how the group met its mandate or challenge.
11. Celebrate the completion of the work.

Educational Uses of Focus Groups

Figure 2.13 illustrates uses and provides examples of focus groups at various levels within education.

Summary

Quality tools, processes, or techniques are designed to extend human capability and effectiveness rather than limit it. They help educators bring people together to solve problems. For these reasons, and others mentioned in Chapter 1, the quality group process tools have been presented prior to the so-called technical quality tools. Although individuals may use any of the tools either at work or at home, these tools are much more powerful when used within groups. Brainstorming and the nominal group technique are free-flowing processes. Focus groups, however, use much more structure, having been given a specific mandate or mission to accomplish. Focus groups are becoming the norm among problem solvers, allowing individuals the advantages of groups in order to utilize numerous quality tools for problem identification and analysis.

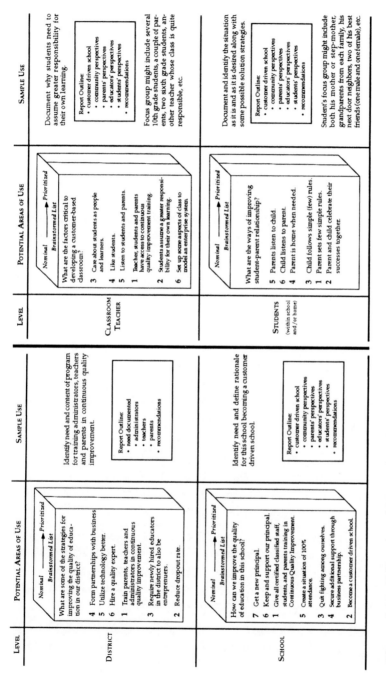

Level	Potential Areas of Use	Sample Use

DISTRICT

Potential Areas of Use — Nominal → Prioritized, Brainstormed List

What are some of the strategies for improving the quality of education in our district?

4 Form partnerships with business.
5 Utilize technology better.
6 Hire a quality expert.
1 Train parents, teachers and administrators in continuous quality improvement.
3 Require newly hired educators in the district to also be entrepreneurs.
2 Reduce dropout rate.

Sample Use: Identify need and content of program for training administrators, teachers and parents in continuous quality improvement.

Report Outline:
• need documented
• administrators
• teachers
• parents
• recommendations

SCHOOL

Potential Areas of Use — Nominal → Prioritized, Brainstormed List

How can we improve the quality of education in this school?

7 Get a new principal.
6 Keep and support our principal.
1 Give all certified classified staff, students, and parents training in Continuous Quality Improvement.
5 Create a situation of 100% attendance.
3 Quit fighting among ourselves.
4 Secure additional support through business partnership.
2 Become a customer driven school.

Sample Use: Identify need and define rationale for this school becoming a customer driven school.

Report Outline:
• customer driven school
• community perspectives
• parents' perspectives
• educators' perspectives
• students' perspectives
• recommendations

CLASSROOM TEACHER

Potential Areas of Use — Nominal → Prioritized, Brainstormed List

What are the factors critical to developing a customer-based classroom?

3 Care about students as people and learners.
4 Like students.
5 Listen to students and parents.
1 Teacher, students and parents have access to continuous quality improvement training.
2 Students assume a greater responsibility for their own learning.
6 Set up some aspects of class to model an enterprise system.

Sample Use: Document why students need to assume greater responsibility for their own learning.

Report Outline:
• customer driven school
• community perspectives
• parents' perspectives
• educators' perspectives
• students' perspectives
• recommendations

Focus group might include several 10th grade students, a couple of parents, two sixth grade students, another teacher whose class is quite responsible, etc.

STUDENTS (within school and/or home)

Potential Areas of Use — Nominal → Prioritized, Brainstormed List

What are the ways of improving student-parent relationship?

5 Parents listen to child.
6 Child listens to parent.
4 Parent is home when needed.
3 Child follows simple (few) rules.
1 Parent sets few simple rules.
2 Parent and child celebrate their successes together.

Sample Use: Document and identify the situation as it is and as it is desired along with some possible solution strategies.

Report Outline:
• customer driven school
• community perspectives
• parents' perspectives
• educators' perspectives
• students' perspectives
• recommendations

Student's focus group might include both his mother or step-mother, grandparents from each family, his next door neighbors, two of his best friends (one male and one female), etc.

Figure 2.13. Educational Uses of Focus Groups at Various Levels

Key Terms and Concepts

Brainstorming. This is a group process that challenges everyone, in a freewheeling and risk-free environment, to generate ideas and to identify problems and solutions.

Cross-functional group. There are many functions and classifications of workers within education (e.g., policy-makers, administrators, instructors, advisors, certified and classified personnel, the PTA, school advisory committees, student body councils, etc.). Sometimes it may be appropriate to work in homogeneous groups, but when the pursuit is quality via CQI, group members need to be selected across functions to ensure broad representation as well as to enrich creativity, strategic thinking, and the use of quality tools.

Focus group. This is usually a cross-functional group with a mandate to complete one aspect of problem identification or analysis within a set period of time. More structured than either brainstorming or the nominal group technique, the focus group actually engages in research and gathers data from various educational stockholders via interviews, testimonials, or questionnaires— whatever produces the greatest involvement and richest information base to meet the group's mandate. The final product is usually in the form of an action report.

"More of the same." If you believe that what you have been doing is right, you will probably try to solve problems by simply doing more of what you have already been doing—more of the same. Quality tools used within cross-functional groups help educators discover new and different ways of meeting challenges.

Nominal group technique (NGT). This is a more formalized process than brainstorming in that it not only identifies lists of ideas or suggestions but also facilitates the expression and collection of total group thinking on a topic or question. Consensus and priority ranking are products of this group process.

Quality tools do not belong only to business. Quality tools no more belong only to business than do computers, the practice of leadership, planning, or having a mission. Quality tools belong to everyone, including educators, parents, and students.

References and Sources for Additional Reading

GOAL/QPC. (1990). Research report: Quality function deployment, a process for translating customer needs into a better product and profit. Methuen, MA: Author.

Kohn, A. (1992). *No contest: The case against competition.* Boston: Houghton Miffin.

Krueger, R. A. (1988). *Focus groups: A practical guide for applied research.* Newbury Park, CA: Sage.

Morgan, D. L. (1988). *Focus groups as qualitative research.* Newbury Park, CA: Sage.

Morgan, J. W., & Talbot, R. P., & Benson, R. M. (1990). *A guide to graphic problem-solving processes.* Milwaukee, WI: ASQC Quality Press.

Murchie, D., & Latta, R. F. (1992). *Conducting opinion surveys: Gathering data and input from educational stakeholders.* Vancouver: B.C. Superintendent's Association.

Senge, P. M. (1990). *The fifth discipline: The art of the learning organization.* New York: Doubleday.

Stewart, D. W. (1990). *Focus group: Theory and practice.* Newbury Park, CA: Sage.

(See also Bonstingl and 3 M Corporation in the Preface.)

✧ 3 ✧

Using the Seven Basic Quality Tools

The significant problems we face today cannot be solved at the same level of thinking we were at when we created them.

ALBERT EINSTEIN

In Chapter 2, we stressed that within the free-flowing and expansionary processes of brainstorming and nominal group technique, few if any other quality tools are utilized. These two tools allow everyone in a group to be involved and to give unstructured, creative input. Focus groups or teams, however, must adapt both quantitative and qualitative techniques to the task of gathering data relative to a specific problem. Members within these smaller units might well utilize some or all of the following seven basic quality tools.

First let us mention that several of the basic quality tools—histograms, pareto charts, scatter diagrams, trend/run charts, and control charts—are also referred to as statistical process control (SPC) tools. SPC is a statistical method for determining the cause of variation using probability theory to control and improve processes. Once the problem is identified, quantifiable data provide reference points or a baseline for problem analysis. A cause-and-effect analysis is then conducted to identify common and special causes of variation so that corrective action may be planned or implemented.

Figure 3.1 introduces the seven basic quality tools. In the text, each tool is supported with an educational scenario, followed by three sections describing the tool, why it is used, and how it can be created. Illustrative educational uses of the process conclude each section.

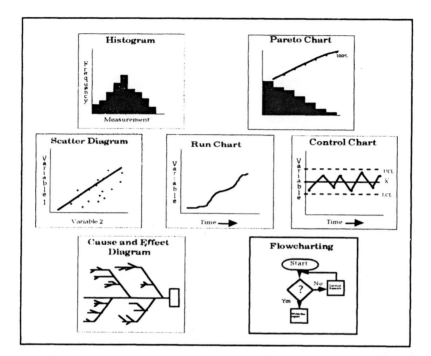

Figure 3.1. The Seven Basic Quality Tools

Histograms

Understanding the What, Why, and How of Histograms

SCENARIO: Low attendance at school has been a problem in the district over the last few years. Members of the focus group ask Bill to take the 1992-1993 data and to graph it for their next meeting. Bill decides to use a simple histogram and puts the following data into the chart in Figure 3.2:

0-5 absences (80 students)   21-25 absences (100 students)
6-10 absences (200 students)   26-30 absences (50 students)
11-15 absences (300 students)   31-35 absences (30 students)
16-20 absences (150 students)   36-40 absences (10 students)
over 40 absences (4 students)

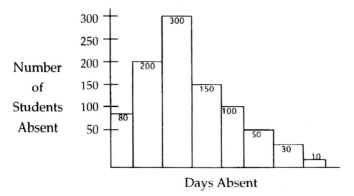

Figure 3.2. District Student Absenteeism: 1992-1993

What Is It?

A *histogram* is a columnar graph showing the frequency distribution of data collected on a given variable. The height of each column displays the frequency (number) of a given measurement. The frequency distribution will indicate grouping of data and how much variation exists. Data is tabulated and arranged according to size.

Why Use It?

Data for a histogram can be gathered about any series of events, a series of occurrences, or a problem that has variant activity. The data help identify changes or shifts in processes as changes are made. This tool helps determine the range of variation and facilitates the establishment of standards on which future measurements can be compared. Data problems may be identified when data classes show abrupt rather than gradual changes. A bimodal shape could indicate inconsistent data collection or a specific problem area.

How Do You Create It?

The following steps are used to create a histogram:

1. Determine measurements to be taken.
2. Collect data.
3. Organize data into incremental units.
4. Determine the range of data (subtract the lowest number from the highest number).
5. Divide the full range into a logical number of data classes (enough columns to provide detail without confusing the reader with irregular columns).
6. Use simple numbers (avoid fractions) to show the width of each class represented by a column (0-9, 10-19, 20-29, etc.).
7. Accumulate the data for each data class and display the frequency by using the appropriate column width.
8. Develop a graph to show summarized results.

Educational Uses of Histograms

Figure 3.3 suggests uses of histograms at various levels with a sample use at each level.

Pareto Charts

Understanding the What, Why, and How of Pareto Charts

SCENARIO: Members of the focus group on attendance computed that there were 924 absences last year. If 100% were unexcused absences, the district has lost 924 × $14 (average daily attendance) = $12,936, which is simply not acceptable. Committee members decided to sort excused and unexcused absences. They found that there were 278 excused absences and calculated the unexcused absences to be 646. Two members of the focus group were then recruited to identify the categories of the unexcused absences and to present them to the group in graphic form at their next meeting. Sharon and Mary accepted the task and later presented the pareto chart shown in Figure 3.4.

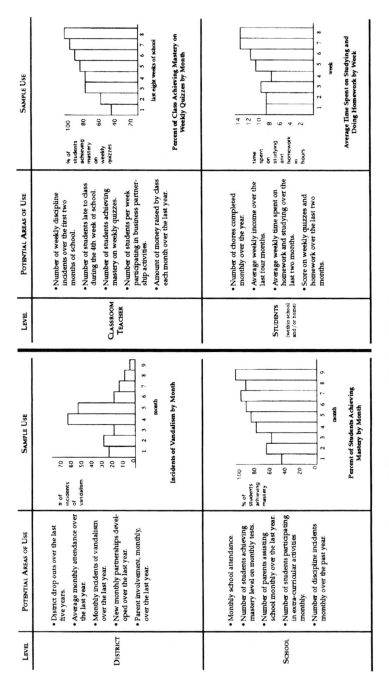

Figure 3.3. Educational Uses of Histograms at Various Levels

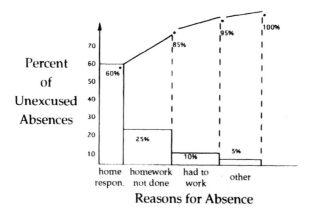

Reasons for Absence

Figure 3.4. Pareto Chart of Reasons for Unexcused Absences

What Is It?

A *pareto chart* is a type of bar chart, prioritized in descending order of magnitude or importance from left to right. It shows at a glance which factors are occurring often most.

The pareto chart is named after a nineteenth-century Italian economist, Vilfredo Pareto. Pareto indicated that 20% of the people have 80% of the wealth. Juran (1989) extended this idea beyond the principle of wealth to problems in general and concluded that

- 80% of all problems can be traced to 20% of all the varied possible causes.
- The remaining 80% of the causes account for only 20% of the problems.

If we work on the 20% of the reasons causing 80% of the problems, we focus our energy on those things that make the most difference. We gain the most by attacking the few critical causes.

Why Use It?

Use this tool when you need to sift the vital few from the trivial many. At a glance you can identify where problems most frequently occur. Look at the number and various types of problems over time in order to locate opportunities for improvement. Further analysis can locate points where problems most likely will occur.

How Do You Create It?

The following steps are taken to create a pareto chart:

1. Select problems or areas to be analyzed.
2. Select standards for comparison or categories into which you want to group the data.
3. Determine the time period of the study.
4. Collect data and total the occurrences in each data category.
5. List categories from left to right on the horizontal axis in descending order—from largest to smallest.
6. Construct a bar graph to display the data. Above each classification draw a rectangle whose height represents the frequency.
7. Calculate cumulative frequencies and percentages.
8. Construct a cumulative line graph.

Having completed the chart, examine the highest categories and begin problem solving using quality tools such as brainstorming, the NGT, and the focus group.

Educational Uses of Pareto Charts

Figure 3.5 suggests uses of pareto charts at various levels with sample uses at each level. The pareto chart is best followed by a cause-and-effect diagram, also known as a fishbone diagram, which is discussed later in this chapter.

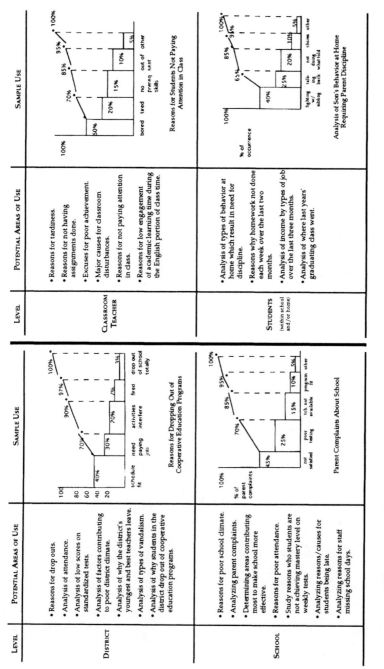

LEVEL	POTENTIAL AREAS OF USE	SAMPLE USE
DISTRICT	• Reasons for drop outs. • Analysis of attendance. • Analysis of low scores on standardized tests. • Analysis of factors contributing to poor district climate. • Analysis of why the district's youngest and best teachers leave. • Analysis of types of vandalism. • Analysis of why students in the district drop out of cooperative education programs.	Reasons for Dropping Out of Cooperative Education Programs
SCHOOL	• Reasons for poor school climate. • Analyzing parent complaints. • Determining areas contributing most to make school more effective. • Reasons for poor attendance. • Study reasons who students are not achieving mastery level on weekly tests. • Analyzing reasons/causes for students being late. • Analyzing reasons for staff missing school days.	Parent Complaints About School

LEVEL	POTENTIAL AREAS OF USE	SAMPLE USE
CLASSROOM TEACHER	• Reasons for tardiness. • Reasons for not having assignments done. • Excuses for poor achievement. • Major causes for classroom disturbances. • Reasons for not paying attention in class. • Reasons for low engagement of academic learning time during the English portion of class time.	Reasons for Students Not Paying Attention in Class
STUDENTS (within school and/or home)	• Analysis of types of behavior at home which result in need for discipline. • Reasons why homework not done each week over the last two months. • Analysis of income by types of job over the last three months. • Analysis of where last years' graduating class went.	Analysis of Son's Behavior at Home Requiring Parent Discipline

Figure 3.5. Educational Uses of Pareto Charts at Various Levels

Scatter Diagrams

Understanding the What, Why, and How of Scatter Diagrams

SCENARIO: After analyzing absenteeism in the district, the focus group members decide to get a handle on the results of absenteeism. Members discuss Sharon and Mary's pareto chart, then ask Bill to join these two in analyzing the test scores of students having more than five absences, regardless of whether they are excused or unexcused. The three eager beavers remain after the others have dispersed and agree to produce a scatter diagram (Figure 3.6).

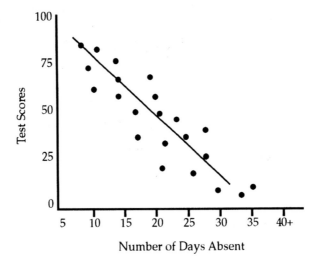

Figure 3.6. Test Scores of Students With Five or More Absences

What Is It?

A *scatter diagram* is a graph that plots one variable against another.

Why Use It?

The scatter diagram is used to test for a cause-and-effect relationship. Properly plotted, it shows the possible relationship, or correlation, between two variables. If a relationship does exist, one cannot conclude that one factor causes the other but must simply note the existence—and, perhaps, the strength—of that relationship. The direction and tightness of a cluster show the strength of the relationship. The more the points/cluster approximates a straight line, the stronger the relationship between the two variables.

How Do You Create It?

The following steps are used to create a scatter diagram:

1. Decide which variables you wish to chart.
2. Prepare a graph with one variable on the vertical axis of the chart and the other on the horizontal axis.
3. Examine the cluster to see if a relationship exists, that is, can a straight line be drawn that approximates the cluster? If necessary, conduct a correlational statistical test.

You may wish to further examine any points totally off the cluster to seek an explanation. For example, are the extreme deviations due to common or special causes?

Educational Uses of Scatter Diagrams

Figure 3.7 contains uses of scatter diagrams at various levels with a sample use at each level.

LEVEL	POTENTIAL AREAS OF USE	SAMPLE USE
DISTRICT	*Look for potential relationships between:* • Aptitude and scores on tests. • Absenteeism and scores on tests. • Parent involvement and school climate. • Average family income and average score on test. • Parent involvement in school activities and child's performance. • Number of years teaching experience and teaching effectiveness.	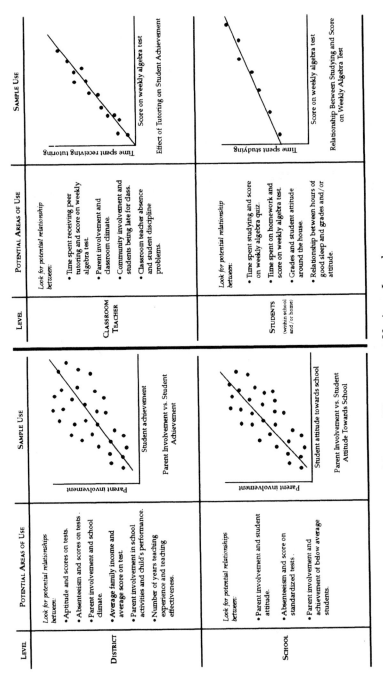 Parent involvement vs. student achievement. *(Parent involvement / Student achievement)* **Parent Involvement vs. Student Achievement**
SCHOOL	*Look for potential relationships between:* • Parent involvement and student attitude. • Absenteeism and score on standardized tests. • Parent involvement and achievement of below average students.	*(Parent involvement / Student attitude towards school)* **Parent Involvement vs. Student Attitude Towards School**

LEVEL	POTENTIAL AREAS OF USE	SAMPLE USE
CLASSROOM TEACHER	*Look for potential relationship between:* • Time spent receiving peer tutoring and score on weekly algebra test. • Parent involvement and classroom climate. • Community involvement and students being late for class. • Classroom teacher absence and student discipline problems.	 *(Time spent receiving tutoring / Score on weekly algebra test)* **Effect of Tutoring on Student Achievement**
STUDENTS (within school and/or home)	*Look for potential relationship between:* • Time spent studying and score on weekly algebra quiz. • Time spent on homework and score on weekly algebra test. • Grades and student attitude around the house. • Relationship between hours of good sleep and grades and/or attitude.	*(Time spent studying / Score on weekly algebra test)* **Relationship Between Studying and Score on Weekly Algebra Test**

Figure 3.7. Educational Uses of Scatter Diagrams at Various Levels

Trend/Run Charts

Understanding the What, Why, and How of Trend/Run Charts

SCENARIO: Over the past 2 years the district has averaged $5000/month extra income through forming business partnerships. It is now the end of the following year and the district opts to use a trend chart to see how monthly income for the past year compares with its overall average and with the 2 previous years. A cross-functional group is established, and it produces the trend chart illustrated in Figure 3.8. A positive trend for this year is clearly indicated.

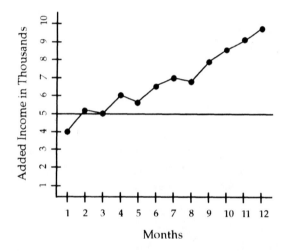

Figure 3.8. Trend Chart of Monthly Income Received Via Business Partnerships

What Is It?

A *trend chart* shows a running tally of some measurable characteristic over time. Trend charts are often referred to as run charts.

Why Use It?

Trend/run charts are useful when there is a system or process important enough to warrant continuous monitoring. For example, if additional income (via partnerships, etc.) is critical to the district, then it warrants monitoring. Imagine what would happen if this income totally disappeared. Small random variations are to be expected, so data points just off the long-range average line may warrant little more than a casual eye. However, several data points off this line running in the same direction might well represent a significant and meaningful change. Figure 3.8 shows a positive trend indeed, as previous partners may be continuing their contributions even as new partnerships are added, thus creating an additive effect for this fortunate district.

How Do You Create It?

The following steps are used to create a trend/run chart:

1. Identify the area of concern.
2. Log the frequency of that concern over time.
3. Chart the frequency or quantity of that concern over time. Time is graphed on the horizontal axis and frequency/quantity is graphed on the vertical axis.

When finished, study the chart to see if there are critical times during which problems of various types occur. Use your knowledge of quality tools to work on these problems.

Educational Uses of Trend Charts

Figure 3.9 suggests uses of trend charts at various levels with a sample use at each level.

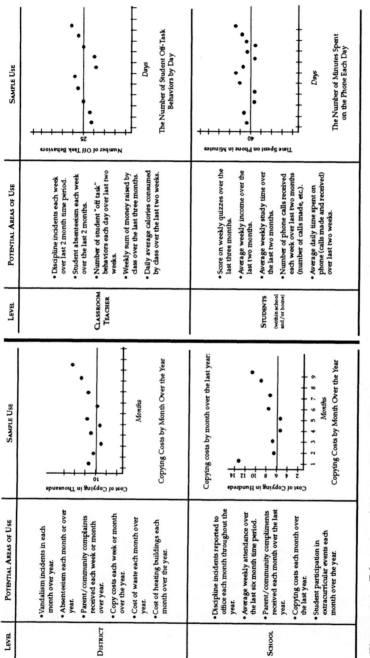

LEVEL	POTENTIAL AREAS OF USE	SAMPLE USE
DISTRICT	• Vandalism incidents in each month over year. • Absenteeism each month or over year. • Parent/community complaints received each week or month over year. • Copy costs each week or month over the year. • Cost of waste each month over year. • Cost of heating buildings each month over the year.	Cost of Copying in Thousands; 10; Months Copying Costs by Month Over the Year
SCHOOL	• Discipline incidents reported to office each month throughout the year. • Average weekly attendance over the last six month time period. • Parent/community compliments received each month over the last year. • Copying costs each month over the last year. • Student participation in extracurricular events each month over the year.	Copying costs by month over the last year. Cost of Copying in Hundreds; 2 4 6 8 9 10 12 14; Months 1 2 3 4 5 6 7 8 9 Copying Costs by Month Over the Year

SAMPLE USE	POTENTIAL AREAS OF USE	LEVEL
Number of Off Task Behaviors; 25; Days The Number of Student Off-Task Behaviors by Day	• Discipline incidents each week over last 2 month time period. • Student absenteeism each week over the last 2 months. • Number of student "off task" behaviors each day over last two weeks. • Weekly sum of money raised by class over the last three months. • Daily average calories consumed by class over the last two weeks.	CLASSROOM TEACHER
Time Spent on Phone in Minutes; 40; Days The Number of Minutes Spent on the Phone Each Day	• Score on weekly quizzes over the last three months. • Average weekly income over the last two months. • Average weekly study time over the last two months. • Number of phone calls received each week over last two months (number of calls made, etc.). • Average daily time spent on phone (calls made and received) over last two weeks.	STUDENTS (within school and/or home)

Figure 3.9. Educational Uses of Trend (Run) Charts at Various Levels

45

Control Charts

Understanding the What, Why, and How of Control Charts

SCENARIO: The district has averaged $5,000 extra monthly income from business partnerships over the past 2 years (1990-1991; 1991-1992) and has come to depend on this income. To ensure or monitor the situation, upper and lower spending limits are established: upper limit = $6,000, lower limit = $4,000. The superintendent decides to model the use of control charts to her leadership team. Using the district's monthly income for the 1992-1993 year, she constructs the control chart contained in Figure 3.10.

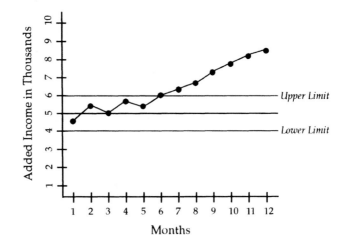

Figure 3.10. Control Chart of 1992-1993 Income Plotted Against 1990-1992 Income's Upper and Lower Limits

What Is It?

A *control chart* is a graphic representation of sequential or time-related performance of a process determined with either practical or statistical upper and lower limits. (If statistically determined, two standard deviations above and below the long-term average will typically be the upper and lower limits.) It is a clear visual display that quickly tells when a process is either "out of control" or a new trend has developed or is in the process of developing.

Why Use It?

A control chart measures actual process performance relative to certain established limits. Control charts show variation on the process variables and seek to identify common rather than special causes of variation. Carefully distinguish between these two types of causes because, if you treat common causes as a special causes or vice versa, you may discard an entire system when all it needed was some fine tuning via the Continuous Quality Improvement process.

How Do You Create It?

The following steps are used to create control charts:

1. Collect data on the issue/concern.
2. Plot data on a control chart.
3. Determine the upper and lower control chart limits either based on experience and what makes sense and/or by establishing two standard deviations from the long-term average, and then add them to the control chart.
4. Identify points outside of the control chart limits.
5. Determine causes of points outside of the control chart limits.
6. Identify ways to eliminate special causes.
7. Identify ways to reduce normal variance (resulting from common causes) within the control chart limits and improve the long-term average (mean).
8. If the long-term average needs to be changed (expectations and/or priorities have changed), change it and reset the upper and lower limits.

Educational Uses of Control Charts

Figure 3.11 suggests uses of control charts at various levels with a sample use at each level.

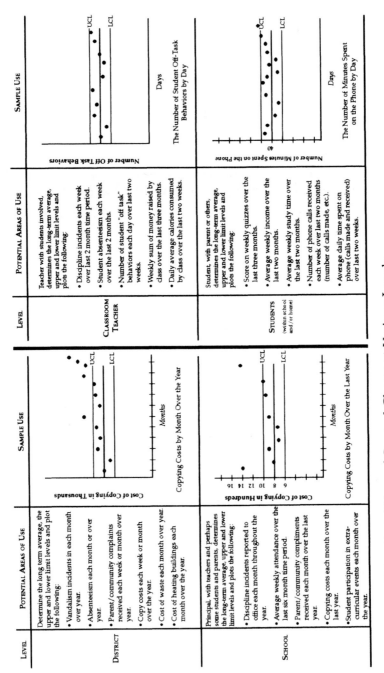

LEVEL	POTENTIAL AREAS OF USE	SAMPLE USE
DISTRICT	Determine the long term average, the upper and lower limit levels and plot the following: • Vandalism incidents in each month over year. • Absenteeism each month or over year. • Parent/community complaints received each week or month over year. • Copy costs each week or month over the year. • Cost of waste each month over year. • Cost of heating buildings each month over the year.	Cost of Copying in Thousands — UCL / LCL — Months — Copying Costs by Month Over the Year
SCHOOL	Principal, with teachers and perhaps some students and parents, determines the long-term average, upper and lower limit levels and plots the following: • Discipline incidents reported to office each month throughout the year. • Average weekly attendance over the last six month time period. • Parent/community compliments received each month over the last year. • Copying costs each month over the last year. • Student participation in extra-curricular events each month over the year.	Cost of Copying in Hundreds — UCL / LCL — 6 8 10 12 14 16 — Months — Copying Costs by Month Over the Last Year

SAMPLE USE	LEVEL	POTENTIAL AREAS OF USE
Number of Off Task Behaviors — UCL / LCL — Days — The Number of Student Off-Task Behaviors by Day	CLASSROOM TEACHER	Teacher with students involved, determines the long-term average, upper and lower limit levels and plots the following: • Discipline incidents each week over last 2 month time period. • Student absenteeism each week over the last 2 months. • Number of student "off task" behaviors each day over last two weeks. • Weekly sum of money raised by class over the last three months. • Daily average calories consumed by class over the last two weeks.
Number of Minutes Spent on the Phone — UCL / LCL — 40 — Days — The Number of Minutes Spent on the Phone by Day	STUDENTS (within school and/or home)	Student, with parent or others, determines the long-term average, upper and lower limit levels and plots the following: • Score on weekly quizzes over the last three months. • Average weekly income over the last two months. • Average weekly study time over the last two months. • Number of phone calls received each week over last two months (number of calls made, etc). • Average daily time spent on phone (calls made and received) over last two weeks.

Figure 3.11. Educational Uses of Control Charts at Various Levels

Cause-and-Effect/Fishbone Diagrams

Understanding the What, Why, and How of Cause-and-Effect/Fishbone Diagrams

Although the first five of the seven basic quality tools are used to look at statistical process control, the last two are pre-planning tools. The cause-and-effect diagram is also known as the fishbone diagram because it resembles the skeleton of a fish. This diagram is sometimes called the Ishikawa chart after an engineer who is a quality guru in Japan.

SCENARIO: Educators representing the district have been brought together to help deal with the problem of school attendance. During the first meeting, group members identify the major categories of the causes of poor attendance or increasing student absence as due to student, staff, system, or outside influences. The group together brainstorms causes within each category and produces the cause-and-effect diagram in Figure 3.12.

What Is It?

A *cause-and-effect/fishbone diagram* is a structured form of brainstorming that graphically shows the relationship of possible causes and subcauses directly related to an identified effect/problem. It is most commonly used to analyze work-related problems.

Why Use It?

This diagram helps you visualize how various separate causes might interact to effect a desired end or a problem. Ishikawa (1985) noted the following benefits:

- The creation process is educational; it gets discussion going and people learn from each other.
- The diagram helps groups focus on the issues involved in solving the problem, thus reducing complaints and irrelevant discussion.

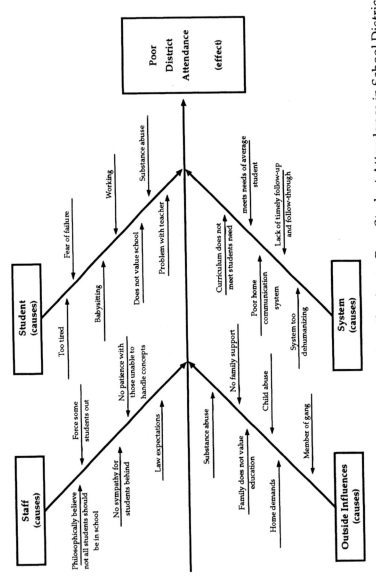

Figure 3.12. Fishbone Diagram of the Causes Contributing to Poor Student Attendance in School District

- Its use results in an active search for the cause of the problem.
- It is used to identify data that can be collected to further the search for the solution to the problem.
- The diagram demonstrates the level of staff understanding—the more complex the diagram, the more sophisticated the understanding of the process.

How Do You Create It?

The following steps are used to create a cause-and-effect/fishbone diagram (see Figure 3.12):

1. Clearly identify the problem to be diagrammed (usually placed in a box at the right of the diagram—"head" of fish).
2. Draw a fishbone structure. Provide ample space to show the factors and their relationships.
3. Identify possible major categories such as methods, people, materials, training, information, and environment.
4. Brainstorm causes of the problem that fall within each of the major categories.
5. As ideas are generated, determine on which branch ("bone") the item should be placed.
6. Note that each branch may have several sub-branches in order to effectively show relationships.
7. Tips on developing the diagram:
   - Develop the diagram as a team.
   - Indicate there is no right or wrong answer.
   - Do not argue or get bogged down—move on.
   - Carry out the breakdowns in enough detail.
   - Get the group to agree on causes.

Educational Uses of Cause-and-Effect/Fishbone Diagrams

Figure 3.13 suggests uses of cause-and-effect/fishbone diagrams at various levels. A sample use for each level is provided in supporting Figures 3.13a, 3.13b, 3.13c, and 3.13d.

(Text continued on page 57)

LEVEL	POTENTIAL AREAS OF USE	SAMPLE USE
DISTRICT	• Causes of poor district attendance. • Reasons for student dropout. • Causes of teacher burnout. • Reasons of parent and community opposition to outcome-based education. • Causes of poor communications within the district. • Reasons for opposition to district implementing continuous quality improvement. • Causes for poor parental involvement throughout district.	See Figure 3.13a. for an example of this tool applied to implementing CQI at the district level.
SCHOOL	• Reasons for low attendance. • Strategies for eliminating school discipline situations. • Strategies for ensuring 100% attendance. • Causes of poor parent and community involvement in school. • Strategies for increasing outside funds. • Reasons why ESL students have problems with social adjustments.	See Figure 3.13b. for an example of this tool applied to the problems that ESL students have with social adjustments.
CLASSROOM TEACHER	• Causes of discipline problems. • Need to increase the number of students reaching mastery on weekly quizzes (100% score). • Causes of students being late. • Strategies for increasing parent and community involvement in class. • Strategies for making the class an enterprise class/environment. • Analysis of why 100% of students do not have a positive attitude about learning.	See Figure 3.13c. for an example of this tool applied to increasing the number of students reaching mastery on weekly quizzes.
STUDENTS (within school and/or home)	• Causes or reasons for being late to school and/or classes. • Reasons for very limited weekly income. • Strategies for improving grade point average from 2.9 to 3.5. • Study reasons why one has so few friends. • Strategies for getting along better with either adults, peers, or siblings.	See Figure 3.13d for an example of this tool applied to the problem of students being late to school and classes.

Figure 3.13. Educational Uses of Fishbone/Cause-and-Effect Diagrams

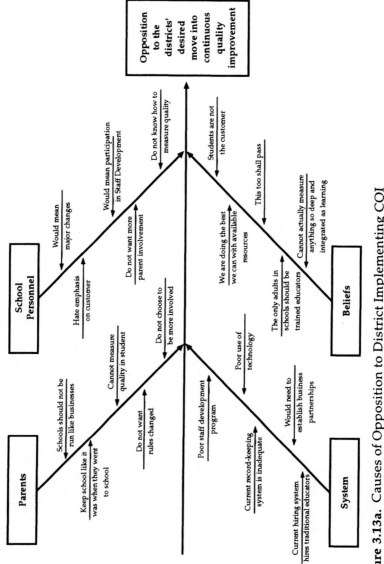

Figure 3.13a. Causes of Opposition to District Implementing CQI

53

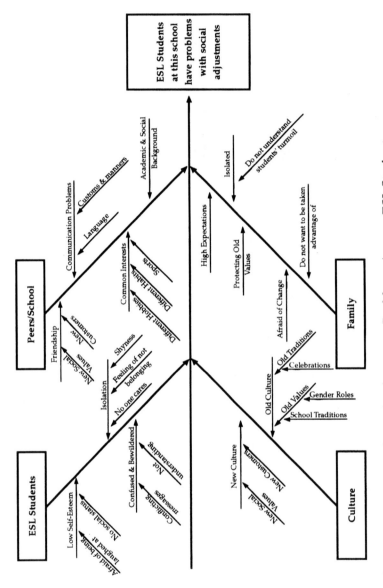

Figure 3.13b. Causes of Social Adjustment Problems Among ESL Students

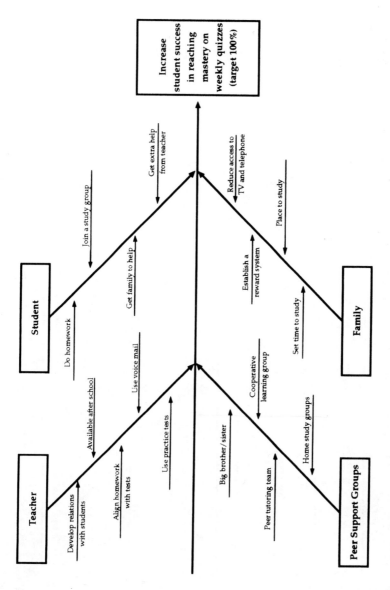

Figure 3.13c. Strategies That Will Cause 100% of Students to Meet or Exceed Mastery of Weekly Quizzes

56

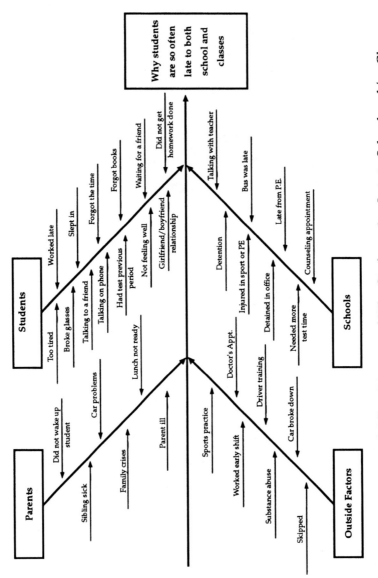

Figure 3.13d. Cause-and-Effect Diagram of Why Students Are Late to School and/or Classes

Flowcharts

Understanding the What, Why, and How of Flowcharts

The flowchart is perhaps the most powerful of the basic tools. It receives this designation because it provides the complete picture of a system or process. As many quality gurus have stated, 85% to 95% of our problems stem from the failure of systems or processes rather than from human inadequacies. Because the flowchart is the best tool for modeling or picturing a system or process, it rightly deserves close attention.

SCENARIO: The district has begun implementing CQI, and a group of high-level administrators are attending a training session on TQM and CQI. This particular day, they are working on quality tools, in particular the flowchart. To get things moving, the facilitator/trainer divides the administrators into triads and asks them to design a flowchart of the photocopying process utilizing only five flowcharting symbols: arrow, rectangle, oblong, diamond, and node or small circle as a connector symbol. The first group finishes and displays the flowchart in Figure 3.14.

What Is It?

A *flowchart* is simply a visual way of charting a process from beginning to end. Symbols are used to represent input from suppliers, sequential work activities, decisions to be made, and output to the customers.

Why Use It?

Flowcharts are a means of analyzing a process. By outlining every step in a process, you can begin to find inefficiencies or problems. You can find steps that may be eliminated and steps to be added. It is a way of pinpointing suboptimization.

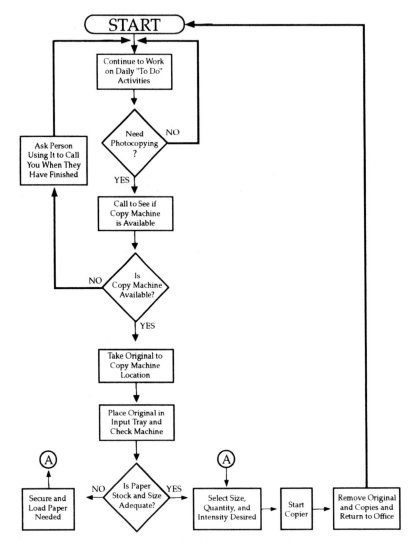

Figure 3.14. Flowchart of the Photocopying Process

How Do You Create It?

The following are the steps for creating flowcharts:

1. Determine the purpose and scope of the flowchart.
2. List all inputs and outputs.
3. Use appropriate flowchart symbols:
   - Keep the use of symbols to a minimum in order to maximize communication.
   - Consider using the five symbols suggested in Figure 3.15, and be consistent.

Symbol	Description	Example
Oblong	Process of System begins or ends..	• Begin attendance system. • Start Needs assessment system. • Begin CQI process. • End grievance procedures. • End grade reporting system.
Rectangle	Operation or activity is performed. Time and resources are spent or consumed in act of doing, analyzing, completing, designing, etc., on operation.	• Write report. • Review and update recommendations. • Conduct survey. • Monitor CQI program. • Establish benchmarks. • Analyze needs assessment data. • Assign grades.
Diamond	Decision point. A point in a process or system where a decision must be made. The decision results in a 'Yes' or 'No' responses with each response flowing to different operations or activities.	•Should the candidate be hired? • Should the program be revised? • Should the program be continued? • Ready for school tomorrow? • Does process meet targets?
Solid Arrow	Direction of flow. Denotes the direction and order or process steps. It also links the activities and classrooms within the system/process. No time or resources are expended as no activity takes place.	• See flowchart figures in this section of the text.
Node	Connector. Connects the operation or decisions without having to cross flow lines thus keeping the resultant flowchart less complex and easier to understand.	• See figures 3.16a and 3.16c in this section of the text.

Figure 3.15. Flowcharting Symbols and Their Uses

4. Don't be concerned about defining the process specifically and completely in the first draft:

- A *macroanalysis* will provide a high-level view of the process.
- A more specific analysis can then be done to provide an intermediate or a highly-detailed picture.

5. Review the flowchart by addressing the following questions. Does the flowchart

- Show proper flow of work/information?
- Show sequential and simultaneous events?
- Show all the potential paths that work/information can take? What about special cases?
- Accurately reflect all major decisions?
- Accurately capture what really happens?

6. Date the chart.

7. Look for steps that are inefficient or unnecessary.

8. Hints on designing:

- Involve other people who are familiar with the process and remember to gain consensus.
- Refrain from trying to change or fix a piece of a process until the process is fully diagrammed and analyzed.

Educational Uses of Flowcharts

Flowcharts may be sequential block diagrams or pictorial models with no decisions represented. To maximize communication, keep things simple and be sensitive to the fact that big and complex ideas may scare away many people. Flowcharts may also be extremely detailed, getting at the real heart of a system or process (i.e., those things that may have to be changed or eliminated for any real improvement to be realized). There is a right time and place both for simplicity and for complexity.

Figure 3.16 suggests several uses of flowcharts at various levels with sample uses at each level. A sample use for each level is shown in supporting Figures 3.16a, 3.16b, 3.16c, and 31.6d.

Level	Potential Uses of Flowcharts	Sample Use
District	• Model teacher hiring process. • Model teacher and/or administrator grievance procedures. • Model student suspension process. • Model needs assessment process. • Model C.Q.I. process. • Model strategic planning process. • Model attendance procedures. • Model process for supervising teachers and/or administrators.	See Figure 3.16a. for an example of this tool applied to modeling a school district's approach to problem solving.
School	• Model of school accreditation process. • Model of daily attendance system. • Model of student grievance procedures. • Model of procedures for fire and earthquake drills. • Model of school budgeting procedures. • Model of grade reporting system.	See Figure 3.16b. for an example of this tool applied to modeling a "school-based" accountability system.
Classroom Teacher	• Model classroom discipline procedures. • Model procedures used with late students. • Model process used to identify students needing special assistance. • Model process for increasing parent and community involvement. • Model process for ensuring that all students meet or exceed mastery on weekly quizzes. • Model process for student participation in cooperative education. • Model process for students selecting independent study to follow.	See Figure 3.16c. for an example of this tool applied to outlining a process for students participating in cooperative education to follow.
Students (within school and/or home)	• Model process designed to guarantee an increase in grade point average. • Model process for increasing weekly income from $10/week to $30/week. • Model process to eliminate tardiness to both school and classes. • Model system to improve popularity. • Model system to improve relationship with parent(s). • Model process for meeting nightly obligations.	See Figure 3.16d. for an example of this tool applied to a student meeting his/her nightly obligations.

Figure 3.16. Educational Uses of Flowcharting at Various Levels

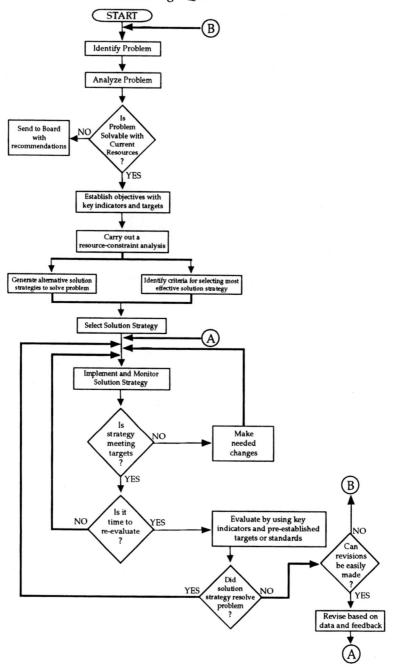

Figure 3.16a. Model of District's Approach to Problem Solving

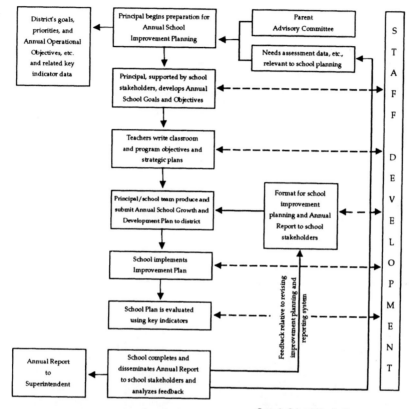

School Site Management Team's
Leadership Ethic: Leadership by Example

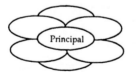

Sample School Key Indicators:

1. Parent and/or Community Involvement
2. Discipline
3. Attendance
4. Substance Abuse
5. Technology
6. Class-size
7. Student Performance
8. Parent Assessment of Quality of Instruction and/or Learning Environment
9. Student Attitude toward School
10. Student Self-Concept

Figure 3.16b. Model of School's Accountability System Utilizing Key Quality Indicators

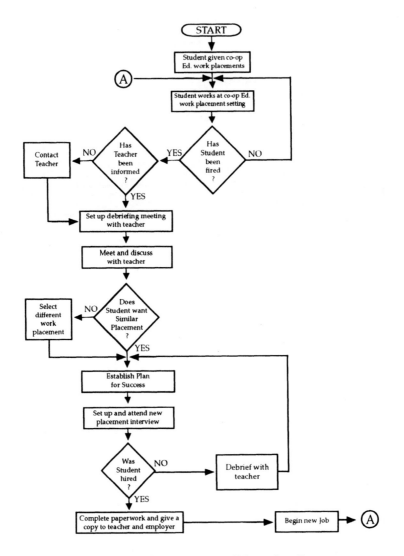

Figure 3.16c. Model of Cooperative Education Process

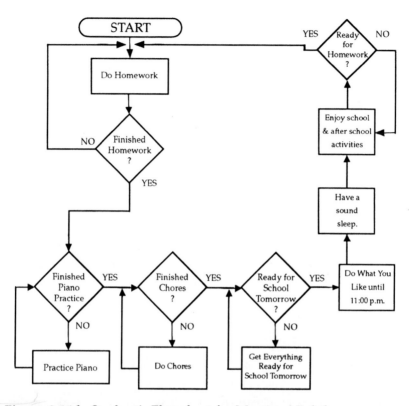

Figure 3.16d. Student's Flowchart for Meeting Nightly Obligations Prior to Enjoying Flexible Time

Summary

Knowing that many educators and taxpayers are visual learners, we believe some pictures may be worth ten thousand words. The seven basic quality tools provide vivid and accurate visuals of actual situations in education. In addition, the tools guide educators to identify and focus on real problems, provide baseline data to evaluate the impact that implemented change might have, and graphically communicate positive outcomes that have

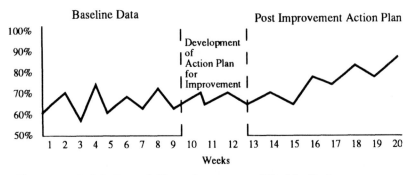

Figure 3.17. Mr. Jones' Class Average on Weekly Quizzes: Before and After the CQI Process

occurred as a result of problem-solving efforts (see Figure 3.17). Imagine the power of being able to communicate your success to the public at large! The quality tools discussed in this chapter empower individuals and groups to choose better directions as well as improve communication.

Key Terms and Concepts

Cause-and-effect/fishbone diagram. This diagram results in an array showing how the various causes of a particular event/problem are clustered and relate to each other.

Control chart. A trend/run chart with set upper and lower limits. Variation that occurs within the established limits is random, expected, and acceptable. Variations outside of the limits are not anticipated or expected and may be due to unique events; in any case, these situations warrant closer examination.

Flowchart. A visual way of diagramming a system or process by linking processes and decisions with flow arrows.

Histogram. A columnar graph or bar chart showing the frequency of occurrence of a measured characteristic of a process.

Monitoring. Closely watching for the expected to occur as planned. Quality tools are often used to graphically monitor systems or planned change efforts. If things do not go as planned, adjustments can be made along the way rather than having to wait until it is too late.

Pareto chart. A histogram showing the major contributors to a problem in descending order (left to right).

Scatter diagram. A scatter diagram is a graph that plots one variable against another to see if any possible relationship exists between the two.

Statistical process control (SPC). The use of statistical techniques to chart and analyze systems or processes for the primary purpose of monitoring efforts. This is a way to continuously improve the quality of systems, processes, and related products.

Suboptimization. A system is made up of numerous smaller subsystems. When a subsystem is permitted to become effective at the expense of the larger system and its other subsystems, suboptimization occurs: one subsystem wins, and the others lose. In CQI, the thrust is toward the larger system becoming more effective, thus creating a win/win situation throughout the entire system and its subsystems.

Trend/run charts. This chart shows a running tally of a measurable characteristic over time and is useful for both highlighting shifts and trends as well as for spotting cycles.

References and Sources for Additional Reading

GOAL/QPC. (1992). *The memory jogger for education: A pocket guide of tools for continuous improvement in schools.* Methuen, MA: Author.

Ishikawa, K. (1985). *What is total quality control? The Japanese way.* Englewood Cliffs, NJ: Prentice-Hall.

Juran, J. M. (1989). *Juran on leadership for quality: An executive handbook.* New York: Free Press.

(See also Bonstingl, Cartin, Johnson, Miller & Krumm, and 3 M Corporation in the Preface.)

✧ 4 ✧

Using the Seven Newer Quality Tools:
A Prelude to Planning and Management

*One man challenged another to an all-day wood chopping contest.
The challenger worked very hard, stopping only for a brief lunch
break. The other man had a leisurely lunch and took several breaks
during the day.*

*At the end of the day, the challenger was surprised and annoyed to
find that the other fellow had chopped substantially more wood
than he had. "I don't get it," he said. "Every time I checked, you
were taking a rest, yet you chopped more wood."*

*"But you didn't notice," said the winning woodsman, "I was
sharpening my ax when I sat down to rest."*

AUTHOR UKNOWN

Chapter 2 discussed the importance of interfacing the use of quality tools with different-sized groups of people. Chapter 3 intro-
duced seven basic quality tools groups can engage for problem
identification and analysis. Because this chapter presents seven
newer quality tools for educators who are beginning efforts to
solve specific problems, the emphasis is more on planning than on
statistical or analytical processes. Groups committing themselves
to the preparation of action or implementation plans in the near
future are likely to use the newer quality tools. Figure 4.1 introduces the reader to the seven newer quality tools.

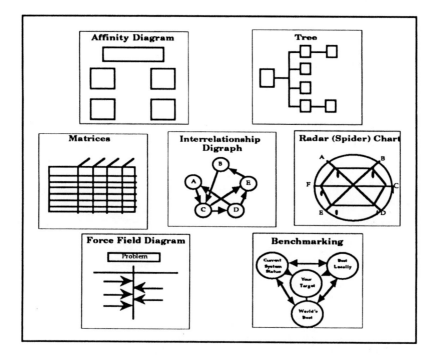

Figure 4.1. The Seven Newer Quality Tools: A Prelude to Planning and Management

Affinity Diagrams

Understanding the What, Why, and How of Affinity Diagrams

SCENARIO: Educators notice that their district has tended to be reactive rather than proactive over the past few years. As a result, the organizational health of the district is at an all-time low. A group of teachers and administrators have just finished brainstorming the question, "How do we keep our employees motivated?" Partial results of the brainstorming are as follows:

- Provide better communication.

- Give opportunity for advancement.
- Provide training.
- Make work meaningful.
- Give good benefits.
- Do not hassle people.
- Pay adequately.
- Be human.
- Focus on mission.
- Give responsibility.
- Reward quickly and appropriately.
- Be fair.
- Supervise positively.
- Give good directions.
- Remove put-downs.
- Provide a clean and cheerful environment.

In order to give more clarity to the list of suggestions, the group members construct an affinity diagram by clustering their suggestions within these five categories: work environment, rewards and recognition, organizational philosophy, job focus, and interpersonal environment. Once the affinity diagram is drafted, they brainstorm further, identifying additional suggestions within each category. The affinity diagram in Figure 4.2 illustrates the group's work thus far.

Prior to the end of the group's meeting, Sharon and Bill offer to prepare a fishbone diagram so that the group can continue further exploration of their suggestions.

What Is It?

The *affinity diagram* is a planning tool used to cluster complex, apparently unrelated data into natural and meaningful groups. In this creative brainstorming process, ideas are grouped according to their natural relationships. Each idea is placed on a separate post-it sheet or notecard.

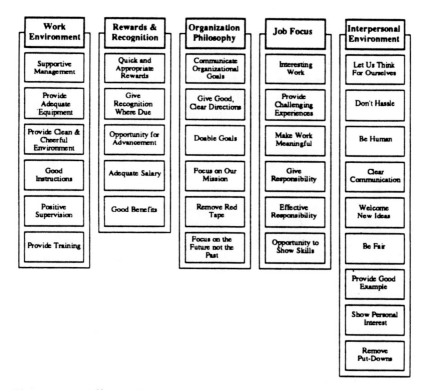

Figure 4.2. Affinity Diagram of Keeping Employees Motivated

Why Use It?

When many ideas are being generated, this tool helps bring order, allowing groups to quickly collect and organize hundreds of ideas. Because everyone is working on the problem, all voices can be heard and all ideas are given equal weight. This tool is very effective when used within the brainstorming process.

How Do You Create It?

The following process is used to create an affinity diagram:

1. After selecting a question or issue to be addressed, write it on a flipchart and post where visible to all participants.

2. Use the brainstorming process (Chapter 2) to generate ideas. Avoid single-word ideas. Print each idea on a separate self-adhesive notecard.

3. Post the notes on a large flat surface without trying to place them in a specific order.

4. To avoid duplication and foster inspiration, each idea should be verbally announced to the participants as the notes are posted.

5. Generate data until participants have exhausted all ideas.

6. Silently move the notes into natural groupings. Notes can be grouped and regrouped by anyone at any time.

7. Once the groupings are determined, discussion is allowed. Minor additional rearranging may occur at this time as the participants clarify their understanding of what has been accomplished.

8. Once the groupings are clear, headers are identified and placed at the top of each grouping.

9. If required for clarity, draw a line around each grouping to indicate the items that "belong" to each header card.

10. For further clarification, the next step might be to construct a fishbone/tree diagram.

Educational Uses of Affinity Diagrams

It is best to use the affinity diagram following brainstorming and/or preceding the process of developing a fishbone diagram. With this in mind, see Figure 4.3 for potential uses at various educational levels.

Tree Diagrams

Understanding the What, Why, and How of Tree Diagrams

SCENARIO: Continuing the scenario outlined for the affinity diagram, let us suppose that the group has completed making suggestions for improving each of the five major categories using

Level	Potential Areas of Use	Sample Use	Level	Potential Areas of Use	Sample Use
District	• Studying reasons why students drop out of school. • Strategies for reducing student drop out. • Reasons for poor school attendance. • Strategies for eliminating unexcused absences. • Reasons for so few school partnerships. • Strategies for improving the number of district and school partnerships. • Reasons for so much resistance to the quality improvement. • Strategies for creating a district-wide climate within which 80% of all educational stakeholders are supportive of continuous quality improvement.	Review the scenario, Figure 4.2 and the directions on how to create or apply this tool. Having done so, you should be able to conceptually apply this tool to any or all this tool to any or all of these potential uses.	Classroom Teacher	(Similar to the uses at both the district and school levels, but restated and directed at the classroom level). • Reasons why students are late to class. • Strategies for eliminating students being late to class. • Strategies for increasing the number of students reaching mastery on the weekly quizzes to 100%.	Review the scenario, Figure 4.2 and the directions on how to create or apply this tool. Having done so, you should be able to conceptually apply this tool to any or all this tool to any or all of these potential uses.
School	• Similar to district level uses, but restated and directed at school situations. • How to make staff meeting more effective. • Why students tend to take the path-of-least resistance in selecting their academic courses. • Why students are not willing to accept more responsibility for their own learning. • Strategies for improving the "Work Ethic" of students. • Reasons for high teacher absences at this school. • Strategies for increasing parent involvement.	Review the scenario, Figure 4.2 and the directions on how to create or apply this tool. Having done so, you should be able to conceptually apply this tool to any or all this tool to any or all of these potential uses.	Students (within school and/or home)	• Strategies for increasing personal income. • Reasons for GPA. • Strategies for getting and keeping friends. • Strategies for rebuilding parent-student conflicts.	Review the scenario, Figure 4.2 and the directions on how to create or apply this tool. Having done so, you should be able to conceptually apply this tool to any or all this tool to any or all of these potential uses.

Figure 4.3. Educational Uses of Affinity Diagrams at Various Levels

a fishbone diagram. In developing a plan for resolving the prob-lem/issue/concern, the group begins the first draft of a tree dia-gram (Figure 4.4).

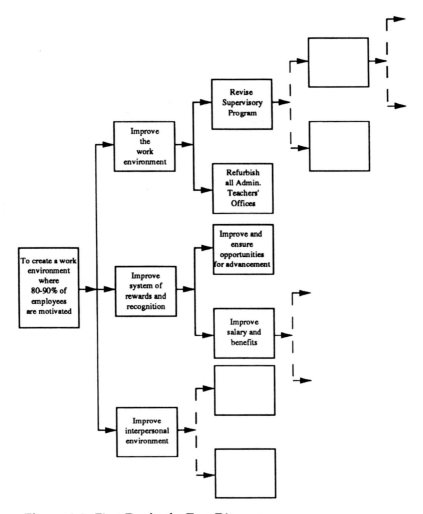

Figure 4.4. First Draft of a Tree Diagram

Recall, if you will, that all the planning and management tools discussed in this chapter are group utilized. Groups usually pro-duce anywhere from two to four drafts before feeling comfortable with their product.

What Is It?

A *tree diagram* is a planning tool used to logically and linearly chart out, in increasing detail, the various tasks that must be accomplished in order to complete a project or achieve a specific objective. It breaks down issues into identifiable components or assignable action items that, when accomplished in sequence, will yield successful attainment of the objective. If a group accomplishes all the detailed subsets of a goal, it is logical that the goal will have been met.

Why Use It?

This is a tool for developing strategies needed to accomplish a major objective. It is also used to successfully identify the root causes of a problem by examining the general problem. Groups may use a tree diagram to delineate their outcomes, competencies, responsibilities, and focus.

How Do You Create It?

The following steps are used to create a tree diagram (Figure 4.4):

1. Assemble a group of people, usually six to eight individuals, who are knowledgeable about the issue/topic and who also are capable of following up with action planning.
2. State the issue (problem or goal) in a box to the left side of a flipchart. Allow ample room to the right of the box for subsequent entries you are about to make.
3. To the right of the box, identify all the broad factors that caused the initial issue.
4. To the right of each broad factor, list the causes behind that factor. Continue this process until the most basic causes of all broad factors have been determined.
5. When the analysis has been developed in as much detail as possible, make a list to the right of the diagram that identifies specific actions needed to accomplish all the factors. This

will eventually accomplish the key objective listed in the initial box.

6. Keep in mind that it is not as important how your tree looks as that it represent the best of the group's thinking and that, if followed and implemented, it will result in the problem/situation's being resolved or the goal's being either met or exceeded.

Educational Uses of Tree Diagrams

A tree diagram is used after a group has completed its problem identification and analysis and selected a priority problem (one which, when resolved, will create the most movement toward quality). The next stage of planning consists of identifying those strategies and activities that will resolve the problem/issue/concern. Figure 4.5 lists only a few of the almost limitless uses of this quality tool.

Matrices

Understanding the What, Why, and How of Matrices

SCENARIO: A district is well into the quality movement, anticipating that CQI will be one of the many benefits of their efforts. However, they have been avoiding even discussing quality tools because many educators in the district have a distaste for measuring, evaluating, or quantifying anything. The board, superintendent, and representatives from certified and classified staff unions meet and give their go-ahead to develop and implement a training program in the seven basic quality tools for all staff. All partners emphasize that the key to meaningful involvement is open and honest communication. A representative group meets with the following results:

1. Five options/alternative solutions to the problem are identified.

LEVEL	POTENTIAL AREAS OF USE	SAMPLE USE
DISTRICT	To identify and develop programs/ action plans to: • Increase funds received from outside the district by 200% • Increase parent and community involvement by 50% district wide. • Increase the number of certified and classified employees who participate in TQM training by 50%. • Improve the district's climate. • Create an environment in which all certified and classified personnel become technologically literate. • Reduce the drop out rate from 30% to 20% in one year and 20-10% by the end of the second year.	Review the scenario, Figure 4.4 and the directions on how to create or apply this tool. Having done so, you should be able to conceptually apply this tool to any or all of these potential uses.
SCHOOL	To identify and develop program(s)/action plans to : • Increase student attendance. • Increase student self-esteem. • Reduce students being late to class. • Raise the school's average score on the districts' math achievement test by a minimum of 5%. • Reduce school vandalism by 70%. • Eliminate office referrals. • Integrate quality into school attitude, performance and outcomes.	Review the scenario, Figure 4.4 and the directions on how to create or apply this tool. Having done so, you should be able to conceptually apply this tool to any or all of these potential uses.
CLASSROOM TEACHER	To identify and develop programs/action plans to: • Improve the climate of the classroom. • Integrate quality into student attitude, performance and products. • Eliminate the need for discipline. • Utilize strategies which empower students to both help themselves and others. • Develop a strong sense of individual responsibility and work ethic in all students. • Increase parent and community involvement. • Raise $4000 to purchase computers and fund an outing for the class.	Review the scenario, Figure 4.4 and the directions on how to create or apply this tool. Having done so, you should be able to conceptually apply this tool to any or all of these potential uses.
STUDENTS (within school and/or home)	To identify and develop programs/action plans to: • Improve their academic grades in all courses by at least one level. • Assist students to manage their time better. • Reduce conflict with adults and their peers. • Keep their room up to their parents' standards. • Improve in their chosen extracurricular activity.	Review the scenario, Figure 4.4 and the directions on how to create or apply this tool. Having done so, you should be able to conceptually apply this tool to any or all of these potential uses.

Figure 4.5. Educational Uses of Tree Diagrams at Various Levels

2. Six quality characteristics against which each option must be measured are identified.

3. A decision to use a linear responsibility guide is made and rough drafts of the charts are developed.

Figures 4.6 and 4.7 represent the rough drafts of the group's work thus far.

What Is It?

A *matrix* is a simple chart, usually two-dimensional, that shows the relationship of several factors along one side (horizontally) with other factors listed along the other side (vertically). It can easily be combined with quality tools such as tree, affinity, or fishbone diagrams to create powerful planning and implementation devices. Three-dimensional matrices, although much more complex, are slowly gaining in popularity because they add depth to the analysis.

Why Use It?

Matrices are useful for prioritizing. They allow each person to see how his or her job relates to the whole process. They encourage everyone to identify and use agreed-on quality characteristics in evaluating proposed solution strategies.

Have you ever noticed that most of our problems in education are perceptual in nature? People "perceive" this to be the problem, or that to be the problem, because they lack information, or are either partially or fully misinformed. Perceptions are symptoms of the effectiveness of a district's or school's communication system. Linear responsibility guides (or matrices) have been with us for almost half of a century and create a model of a communication system specific to a particular program or project. What a powerful and needed tool!

When you buy property, you think "location, location, location." When you utilize quality tools within group processes, think "communication, communication, communication." Like all quality tools, however, the effectiveness and usefulness of matrices depend entirely on how they are used.

Alternative Solutions/Choices	Cost	Acceptability to Board	Effectiveness	Acceptability to Certified and Classified Staff	Time to Get Started	Time to Implement	Total	Rank
A. Hire Consultant/Trainer	Moderate 2	Moderate 2	Moderate 2	Low 1	Low (Easiest) 4	Moderate 2	13	3
B. Purchase and Deliver Packaged Program	Moderate 2	Low 1	Low 1	Low 1	Moderate 2	Moderate 2	9	5
C. Develop Own Program with Involvement of Stakeholder Groups	High 1	High 3	Moderate 2	High (Best) 4	High 1	Moderate 2	13	3
D. Partnership with Adjacent district, Hire Trainer, and Deliver Program Jointly	Low 3	High 3	Moderate 2	Moderate 2	Low 3	Moderate 2	15	2
E. Partnership with a Local Business Already Into TQM, Develop and Deliver Program with Involvement of Stakeholder Groups.	Low (Best) 4	High (Best) 4	High (Best) 4	High 3	High 1	Moderate 2	18	1
	Best = 4 Low = 3 Mod. = 2 High = 1	Low = 1 Mod. = 2 High = 3 Best = 4	Low = 1 Mod. = 2 High = 3 Best = 4	Low = 1 Mod. = 2 High = 3 Best = 4	Best = 4 Low = 3 Mod. = 2 High = 1	Best = 4 Low = 3 Mod. = 2 High = 1		

Figure 4.6. Alternative Solutions Strategies Evaluated Using Quality Characteristics/Indicators

79

Tasks/Activities	School Board	Superintendent	Staff Development Coordinator	Site Based Training Teams	Principal	Certified Staff Union	Teacher Association
Approve Program	C	G	I				
Bring All Players Together	I	C	G/O	I	I	I	I
Develop Program		I	G	O		I	I
Implement Program		I	G	O	I	I	I
Evaluate Program	I	C	G/O	I	I	I	I
Revise Program Based on Feedback		I	G	O		I	I
Make Go-No-Go Decision for Next Year	G	C	C	C	C	C	C

Key: G = General/Coordinating Responsibility
O = Operating Responsibility (Actually does task or function)
C = Must be Consulted
I = Must be Informed

Figure 4.7. Linear Responsibility Guide for Implementing Alternative E in Figure 4.6

How Do You Create It?

Following are the steps for creating a matrix:

1. Assemble a representative group of from six to eight individuals. Make sure that two or three members of the group have experience with quality tools, particularly with matrices.
2. Decide on how the matrix is to be used:
   - Prioritizing
   - Identifying responsibilities
   - Denoting communication systems
   - Other
3. Suppose that the group and its intended uses are those illustrated in the scenario introducing the matrix as a quality tool. Table 4.1 suggests the steps the group may have followed in arriving at Figures 4.6 and 4.7.

TABLE 4.1 Steps for Developing Matrices

Steps to Create Prioritizing Matrix	*Steps to Create Responsibility Guide*
Identify alternative solutions to the problem and list them on left side of matrix.	Identify major tasks/activities and list them on left side of matrix.
Identify the quality characteristics and place them on the top of the matrix.	Identify key individuals and/or groups who will be assuming major responsibilities and who need to be involved in the communication system.
Develop a system for evaluating/measuring or determining the relationship between the alternatives and each of the quality characteristics: low, moderate, high best; or best low, moderate, high.	Develop a key for assigning responsibility or denoting the need for involvement or communication. (In the scenario illustration: G = general responsibility; O = operating responsibility; C = must be consulted; and I = must be informed. A group may choose either a more simplified or complex system.)
Determine the relationship between a quality characteristic and all of the alternatives. The agreed-on value is then placed in the appropriate box within the matrix.	Discuss and jointly compile the matrix. There may be more than one symbol in each box. Note: The responsibility guide works well in conjunction with either a Gantt chart or an arrow diagram.
Continue until the matrix is completed.	
Decide on a point system for converting value judgments to a numerical value. (In the scenario example, two conversion scales are used: (a) high = 3,	

TABLE 4.1 (Continued)

moderate = 2, low = 1; (b) low
= 3, moderate = 2, high = 1.
The best or most ideal value
received is 3+1 = 4 points.)

Place the numerical values in
the lower right corner of each
box in the matrix.

Total the numbers across
each row.

Rank the alternatives. The
option/solution strategy with
the most points is ranked 1,
next most points is ranked 2,
and so on. (In the scenario,
Figure 4.6, alternative E received 18 points and thus
appears to be the most
acceptable strategy based
on the group's quality
characteristics.)

Educational Uses of Matrices

Matrices, like most quality tools, provide a model of the big
picture and are valuable at all levels of education. Figure 4.8
suggests uses of matrices at various levels so that the reader can
visualize potential uses.

Interrelationship Digraphs

Understanding the What, Why, and How
of Interrelationship Digraphs

SCENARIO: A district, beginning its venture into TQM, has
found the going very tough. For this reason, the superintendent

Level	Potential Areas of Use	Sample Use
District	Analyzing and Prioritizing alternative Solution strategies relative to: • Programs for reducing dropouts. • Programs for improving school attendance. • Programs for identifying and assisting high risk students. • Programs for reducing vandalism. • Strategies for reducing teacher and administration absenteeism. • Strategies for improving the relationship between the district administration and the teachers' association. • Programs for improving the districts' climate.	Review the scenario, Figure 4.6 and 4.7, and the directions on how to create or apply this tool. Having done so, you should be able to conceptually apply this tool to any or all of these potential uses.
School	Analyzing and Prioritizing alternative Solution strategies relative to: • Selecting and Implementing a sex education program and keeping parents informed. • Programs for maximizing parent and community relations and communications. • Programs for improving the relationship between the principal and teacher. • Programs for implementing outcome based education and keeping parents involved and informed. • Selecting and implementing a program on AIDS.	Review the scenario, Figure 4.6 and 4.7, and the directions on how to create or apply this tool. Having done so, you should be able to conceptually apply this tool to any or all of these potential uses.
Classroom Teacher	Analyzing and Prioritizing alternative Solution strategies relative to: • Selecting an appropriate program/approach to sex education. • Selecting computers and/or technology • Selecting software. • Fund raising. • Improving the communications and relations between: teachers - students, teacher - parents, and student - parents. • Improving student self-esteem.	Review the scenario, Figure 4.6 and 4.7, and the directions on how to create or apply this tool. Having done so, you should be able to conceptually apply this tool to any or all of these potential uses.
Students (within school and/or home)	Analyzing and Prioritizing alternative Solution strategies relative to: • Increasing personal income 100% per month. • Determining which college or university to attend. • Selecting a study partner. • Selecting which extra-curricular activities to focus on. • Purchasing a car. • Purchasing a computer.	Review the scenario, Figure 4.6 and 4.7, and the directions on how to create or apply this tool. Having done so, you should be able to conceptually apply this tool to any or all of these potential uses.

Figure 4.8. Educational Uses of Matrices at Various Levels

83

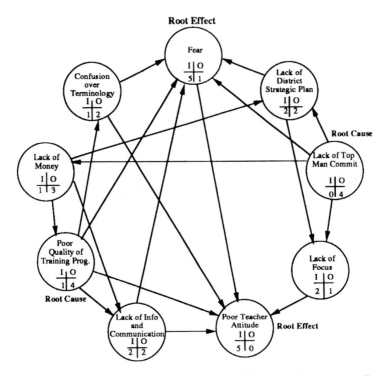

Figure 4.9. Interrelationship Diagram of Barriers Impacting the Implementation of TQM in the District

convenes a district representative group to identify and examine problems and concerns. Members of the group meet, brainstorm, complete a fishbone diagram, and study the interrelationships among what they conclude are the major problems by constructing Figure 4.9, an interrelationship digraph (or relations diagram). Fear and poor teacher attitude toward TQM primarily exist due to the lack of top management commitment and the perceived poor quality of the TQM training program.

What Is It?

An *interrelationship digraph* is a planning tool that presents a pictorial representation of the cause-and-effect relationships among the elements of a problem or issue.

Why Use It?

It is used for examining the more complex problems of cause and effect. By diagramming the relationships, the interactions surface. One can identify root causes and effects and study these relationships among many aspects of issues/problems.

How Do You Create It?

The following steps are used to create an interrelationship digraph (see Figure 4.9):

1. Identify the issue or problem.
2. Construct the diagram by placing the problem in the middle.
3. Take the issues/barriers/causes from either a fishbone or an affinity diagram and place them on header cards. Place the header cards, with their headings, around the problem in a circular pattern.
4. Analyze the relationships—which category influences which other categories. If no relationship exists, no line is drawn.
5. Determine which way the arrow head should go and draw it on one end of the line. The head shows effect. A line can have only one head.
6. Count the number of arrows going in and out of each box and place that number by each box.
7. Identify root causes and effects. The root causes have the greatest number of arrows going out of boxes and root effects have the greatest number of arrows going into boxes.

Next, study the final diagram and plan activities to address root causes, using the quality tools from this book. For example, study how to reduce fear using a tree diagram; plan how to improve a training program using a tree or matrix diagram; or design strategies for ensuring top management buy-in, commitment, and involvement using either a tree or matrix diagram.

Educational Uses of Interrelationship Digraphs

The interrelationship digraph is used infrequently in educational circles. Not only are few people aware of its existence, but some who are aware feel it can quickly become too complex. However, with resources in education becoming more scarce, educators are pressed to spend what little money they have on solutions that will produce the greatest return on their investment.

Figure 4.10 suggests several uses of interrelationship digraphs at various levels.

Radar/Spider Charts

Understanding the What, Why, and How of Radar/Spider Charts

SCENARIO: A district has been into TQM at all levels for 4 years. The superintendent and school board are convinced that they have an award-winning school district. The superintendent brings a representative group together, adding a person from each of two business-in-partnership programs within the district. Group members meet and decide to evaluate the district relative to the Malcolm Baldridge Criteria: leadership, customer focus, strategic quality planning; information and analysis; human resource development and management, management of process quality, and quality and operational results.

Working together, they design an instrument to assess the current status of the district's goal to reach 100% on each of these seven criteria and gather data to produce a radar/spider chart of their findings (Figure 4.11).

What Is It?

The *radar/spider chart* is a tool that gives a graphic picture of how something measures against several criteria or factors.

Level	Potential Areas of Use	Sample Use
District	Analyzing and Studying the potential barriers to: • Reducing absenteeism. • Reducing student dropouts. • Improving the district's public relation program. • Reducing the opposition to outcome based education. • Reducing the friction between the teachers and the school board. • Reducing the tension surrounding TQM. • Reducing class size. • Increasing class size. • Increasing the number of business partnerships.	Review the scenario, Figure 4.9, and the directions on how to create or apply this tool. Having done so, you should be able to conceptually apply this tool to any or all of these potential uses.
School	Analyzing and Studying the potential barriers to: • Reducing the attendance problem. • Increasing the number of students assuming responsibility for their own learning. • Having 100% attendance. • Having 1 computer per 3 students. • Having 100% of the certified and classified staff computer literate. • Increasing parent-community involvement. • Doubling funding received from business and industry. • Improving the education of all special education children.	Review the scenario, Figure 4.9, and the directions on how to create or apply this tool. Having done so, you should be able to conceptually apply this tool to any or all of these potential uses.
Classroom Teacher	Analyzing and Studying the potential barriers to: • Eliminating discipline problems. • Eliminating students being late to class. • Doubling the number of students attaining mastery on the weekly quizzes. • Having the class run a small profit-making business. • Improving classroom climate. • Purchasing eight more computers.	Review the scenario, Figure 4.9, and the directions on how to create or apply this tool. Having done so, you should be able to conceptually apply this tool to any or all of these potential uses.
Students (within school and/or home)	Analyzing and Studying the potential barriers to: • Improving relations with parents. • Improving relations with teachers. • Improving relations with peers. • Getting to school on time 100%. • Improving monthly income. • Improving G.P.A. • Having more friends. • Having own phone, TV, and pager. • Having own car. • Moving out and living with significant other.	Review the scenario, Figure 4.9, and the directions on how to create or apply this tool. Having done so, you should be able to conceptually apply this tool to any or all of these potential uses.

Figure 4.10. Educational Uses of Interrelationship Digraphs at Various Levels

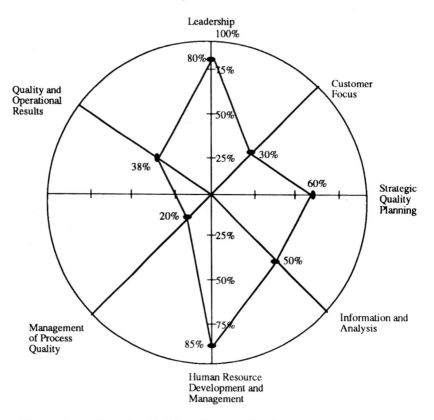

Figure 4.11. A Radar/Spider Chart of the District's Status Measured Against the Baldrige Criteria

Why Use It?

Circular diagrams tend to focus vision and thinking patterns. The radar/spider diagram gives a circular picture in which any distortions become very graphic. This diagram leaves no doubt about what is happening, what is being overachieved, what is being underachieved, and how close you might be to your goal. It is also an excellent tool to utilize within the benchmarking process.

How Do You Create It?

The radar/spider diagram is charted using the following steps (see Figure 4.11):

1. Bring a representative group together.
2. Examine the problem/situation and make sure that the radar/spider diagram is an appropriate tool.
3. Establish the criteria, characteristics, or factors to be measured and charted.
4. Establish the measurement scale to be utilized.
5. Develop the measurement and data collection tools and processes.
6. Gather data and plot findings relative to each criteria on the diagram.
7. Join dots on the barrier axes.
8. Examine shapes and distortions.

When finished, examine the shape and distortions within the diagram to identify both areas of strengths and those that require greater effort and focus.

Educational Uses of Radar/Spider Diagrams

The radar/spider diagram is particularly useful when comparing one district, school, or program with another. Figure 4.12 shows potential uses of radar/spider diagrams.

Force-Field Analysis

Understanding the What, Why, and How of Force-Field Analysis

SCENARIO: District representatives have found a great deal of resistance in implementing their TQM philosophy and program. As a matter of fact, they are stuck and have not made any progress over the last few months. The superintendent asks a small group of six to eight people to study this situation. They utilize several quality tools: affinity diagram, fishbone chart, and interrelationship digraph. Still, the superintendent, the board, and the group are at a loss to resolve the situation. In a final effort, Jackie and Jennifer, two group members, offer to facilitate the group in constructing a force-field analysis of the situation. Members later present the

LEVEL	POTENTIAL AREAS OF USE	SAMPLE USE	LEVEL	POTENTIAL AREAS OF USE	SAMPLE USE
DISTRICT	• Measuring and plotting districts' organizational health or climate. • Measuring and comparing district's climate with climate of another district similar in size and composition, etc. • Measuring and plotting how the public views the school district on several criteria. • Measuring and plotting the districts' status using the Baldrige criteria. • Measuring and plotting the districts' progress toward meeting Deming's 14 organizational characteristics. • Measuring and plotting the districts' progress toward the eight criteria for the President's Award for Quality and Productivity Improvement. • Measuring and plotting the districts' progress and status in meeting Juran's 10 steps to quality improvement. • Measuring the district's status toward becoming an effective school district using agreed upon criteria.	Review the scenario, Figure 4.11, and the directions on how to create or apply this tool. Having done so, you should be able to conceptually apply this tool to any or all of these potential uses.	CLASSROOM TEACHER	• Measuring and diagramming test scores of groups of students: gifted, above average, average, below average, special education, etc. • Measuring and diagramming classroom fund raising activities. • Measuring and diagramming discipline problems by type of problem. • Measuring and diagramming the test scores of the five students in most need of improvement. • Measuring and diagramming the classroom climate. • Measuring and diagramming the effectiveness/quality of the class utilizing five agreed upon key quality indicators.	Review the scenario, Figure 4.11, and the directions on how to create or apply this tool. Having done so, you should be able to conceptually apply this tool to any or all of these potential uses.
SCHOOL	• Measuring and diagramming school climate. • Plotting and comparing the performance of several schools with each other. • Diagramming the funds raised by each grade level by fund raising activity. • Measuring and evaluating the school using the Baldridge criteria. • Measuring student participation, by grade, in academic fair or athletic function. • Measuring parent/community involvement by grade level.	Review the scenario, Figure 4.11, and the directions on how to create or apply this tool. Having done so, you should be able to conceptually apply this tool to any or all of these potential uses.	STUDENTS (within school and/or home)	• Measuring and diagramming income by job. • Measuring and diagramming how time is spent between work, school, studying, TV, friends, etc. • Doing a self-evaluation using selected personality traits. • Doing a self-evaluation regarding attributes for getting and keeping friends. • Measuring and diagramming your current status regarding selected 'life skills'.	Review the scenario, Figure 4.11, and the directions on how to create or apply this tool. Having done so, you should be able to conceptually apply this tool to any or all of these potential uses.

Figure 4.12. Educational Uses of Radar/Spider Diagrams at Various Levels

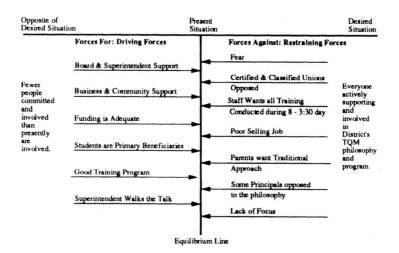

Figure 4.13. Force-Field Analysis of District's TQM Situation

analysis (see Figure 4.13) and accompanying suggestions to the superintendent for possible action.

What Is It?

Force-field analysis is a group creative-thinking process used to identify the forces that either promote or inhibit change. It is a problem-solving tool to help change occur and to identify potential solution strategies. It was designed by Kurt Lewin, Professor at the University of Iowa during World War II and was used to determine people's preferences. Lewin found change to be a struggle between forces. He defined driving forces as those existing forces that help change occur and restraining forces as those that block change.

Why Use It?

This is a strategic tool for change. It identifies driving forces that promote change and restraining forces that inhibit change. It can move a group toward deciding whether to focus on removing restraining forces or strengthening driving forces. Force-field analysis provides a starting point for action and helps encourage creative thinking about the desired change. It is the task of the group to agree on the priorities and choose whether to increase the driving forces, decrease the restraining forces, or do both. Experience suggests that the easiest direction for change is to reduce restraining forces.

How Do You Create It?

A force-field analysis is conducted using the following steps:

1. State the topic; clearly write and underline it at the top of a flip chart or board; and draw a large "T," as in Figure 4.13.
2. Under the topic heading, write "Driving Forces" or "Forces For" on the left side and "Restraining Forces" or "Forces Against" on the right side.
3. Have participants identify driving and restraining forces that affect the topic. Record all forces on the flip chart or board in large enough text for everyone to see.
4. When all forces have been recorded, the group (or subgroups) should review each of the forces listed and brainstorm ideas for strengthening the driving forces and for reducing the restraining forces.
5. If the group is willing, next consider
   a. *Ranking the forces.* (The forces, regardless of whether "for" or "against," would be ranked from 1 to 13 in Figure 4.13.) Forces are ranked by asking the question "Which one force, if changed, would create the most movement toward our goal?" The number 1 is placed above the force. The question is then repeated and the number 2 is placed above the force that, if changed, would create the next greatest movement toward the goal. This process continues until all of the forces have been ranked. For example, the number 1 force might be *Fear* and the number 2 force could be *Board-Superintendent Support.*

b. *Rating the forces on difficulty to change.* Group members simply discuss each force, regardless of its ranking, and rate their perception of how difficult it would be to change (e.g., easy, moderate, or difficult). For illustrative purposes, suppose that the force *Fear* was rated difficult to change and that the force *Board-Superintendent Support* was determined easy to change. The ratings and rankings for each force can be inserted above each force arrow in parentheses; e.g., *Fear (1, difficult), Board-Superintendent Support (2, easy).*

c. *Assessing clarity.* Another consideration open to the group is assessing the clarity of each force. In this situation, members discuss how clear it is to them that a force is really a force. Forces that the group find to be unclear are open to further study via uses of other quality tools. The group's perception of clarity is also placed above each force arrow; e.g., *Fear (1, difficult, clear), Board-Superintendent Support (2, easy, clear).*

d. *Prioritizing actions.* The group can now focus further problem solving and planning on forces that are ranked high, easy to moderate to change, and clear. Highly-ranked forces that are difficult to change and/or unclear should be studied further, possibly using a fishbone diagram.

6. More often than not, a solution strategy involves a combination of forces. When prioritizing actions, the group must also consider what the likely consequences will be. If the result of increasing a driving force is likely to create a corresponding increase in a restraining force, the result will be increased tension without the desired change.

Educational Uses of Force-Field Analysis

Every situation in education, as in life, can be represented as existing within a field of forces. Every problem can therefore be studied via force-field analysis. Figure 4.14 contains problems/situations for which force-field analysis is an appropriate tool.

LEVEL	POTENTIAL AREAS OF USE	SAMPLE USE
DISTRICT	Diagramming the driving and restraining forces surrounding the following challenges / situations: • Low student attendance. • High drop out rate. • Low district climate. • Teacher unrest surrounding accountability. • Staff resistance to TQM. • Parent uneasiness with Outcome-Based Education. • Teacher uneasiness with 'listening to the customer.' • Parent uneasiness with alternative assessment. • Resistance to implementing a district's strategic plan. • Resistance of schools to venture into School Based Strategic Planning.	Review the scenario, Figure 4.13. and the directions on how to create or apply this tool. Having done so, you should be able to conceptually apply this tool to any or all of these potential uses.
SCHOOL	Diagramming the driving and restraining forces surrounding the following challenges / situations: • Teacher dissatisfaction with staff meetings. • Why student tardiness has not changed. • Why the school drop out rate remains unchanged. • Why so few parents and community members, physically, assist the school. • Why the school grounds are so littered with junk each day. • Why teachers resist the implementation of peer coaching. • Why teachers are not willing to participate in efforts to develop a school based strategic plan aligned with the district's plan. • Why teachers resist using input from students in resolving school problems.	Review the scenario, Figure 4.13. and the directions on how to create or apply this tool. Having done so, you should be able to conceptually apply this tool to any or all of these potential uses.

LEVEL	POTENTIAL AREAS OF USE	SAMPLE USE
CLASSROOM TEACHER	Diagramming the driving and restraining forces surrounding the following challenges / situations: • Why discipline remains a problem. • Why tardiness remains a problem. • Why so many students turn in their homework so late. • Why parent involvement in the class has remained unchanged over the past two years. • Why 30% of the class does not reach the mastery level on weekly quizzes. • Why very few of the below average students ask questions.	Review the scenario, Figure 4.13. and the directions on how to create or apply this tool. Having done so, you should be able to conceptually apply this tool to any or all of these potential uses.
STUDENTS (within school and / or home)	Diagramming the driving and restraining forces surrounding the following challenges / situations: • Why parents do not trust me more. • Why my big brother dislikes me so much. • Why my personal income remains at $7.00 a week. • Why 20% of my homework is turned in late. • Why my teacher does not appear to like me. • Why my weekly average on my science tests remains at 71% when I would like it to be 90%. • I would like to be a teacher when I grow up.	Review the scenario, Figure 4.13. and the directions on how to create or apply this tool. Having done so, you should be able to conceptually apply this tool to any or all of these potential uses.

Figure 4.14. Educational Uses of Force-Field Analysis at Various Levels

Benchmarking

Understanding the What, Why, and How of Benchmarking

SCENARIO: A K-12 district with 10,000 students has used quality tools and identified student drop-out to be one of three top
priority problems. The district chooses to view and accept this
situation as a challenge rather than a problem. The superintendent has called a representative group of six to eight people
together to begin action planning. After some discussion, the
group members unanimously agree to establish a measurably-
stated objective or goal, but not via the usual process of guessing.
Instead, they decide to benchmark the drop-out situation and to
set their target based on this analysis. In brief, they identify the
district in the country with the lowest drop-out rate and calculate
their average, and they also accurately determine the drop-out
rate of their own district. In addition to collecting the data, representatives from this group personally visit the other schools to
carefully study the systems and processes that contribute most to
the lower drop-out rates. Members summarize their findings and
present them along with their recommendations to the superintendent in the form of Figure 4.15 and Figure 4.16.

What Is It?

Benchmarking is a process for analyzing a situation by

1. Identifying what the best to date is, what the average of the
   best is that has been accomplished in three to five other
   situations similar to yours, and what your situation is relative to the challenge; both realistic and stretch targets for the
   improvement objective can be established during this process
2. Visiting and studying systems and processes used by others
   that have been identified as being the best

Why Use It?

Most targets for improvement objectives (improvement targets)
are either blindly set or set, for example, by merely contacting

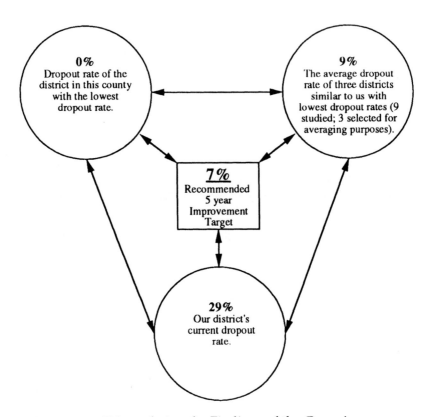

Figure 4.15. Triangulating the Findings of the Group's Benchmarking Process for Establishing the District's Improvement Goal/Objective for the Dropout Situation

others in a similar situation and, if they are doing better, simply adding a few percentage points to what they are achieving. Either way, the process is almost akin to the blind leading the blind. With benchmarking, a great deal of research goes into identifying the very best performance (regardless of size characteristics of the district) and the best three to five situations in districts similar in size and other characteristics to yours. Therefore, improvement targets and annual milestones are established with full knowledge of what is viable. Although this more than warrants the practice of benchmarking in education, the added benefit derives from

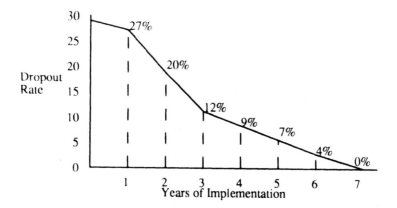

Figure 4.16. Graph Showing Annual Milestones or Subtargets

visiting the best districts and studying the systems, procedures, and processes that you and they feel contribute most to their success. Now a stretch target can be set and promising systems, procedures, and processes can be changed or developed.

How Do You Create It?

The benchmarking process involves the following steps:

1. Select the situation to be benchmarked.
2. Obtain board and superintendent acceptance and commitment.
3. Select a benchmarking team consisting of six to eight people, making sure that some of those selected have a technical background and others have a great deal of credibility throughout the district or school (or whatever level is appropriate for the situation).
4. Train group members in benchmarking and have them utilize quality tools and processes by studying and analyzing the situation being benchmarked. Baseline your own performance.
5. Identify the internal and external customers involved in the situation.

6. Identify the *best* performance of any district (or school, classroom, etc.); identify the best-performing three to five districts similar to yours.

7. Develop action plans for visiting and benchmarking these districts and for analyzing the systems and processes contributing most to their success/effectiveness.

8. Have one or two group members visit the best district, following the action plan established in the preceding step and keeping their eyes and ears open. Keep a journal containing accurate notes on systems and processes. Audiotape or videotape the visit to share with those who are unable to make the trip or who are outside the benchmarking team.

9. Compare your system's performance with those visited. Then triangulate, analyze, discuss, dream, and stretch to establish goals—but not so far that there is absolutely no hope of reaching the target.

10. Establish a target for the improvement objective, and establish annual milestones by which to gauge weekly, monthly, and annual progress.

11. Develop and submit a report to the superintendent (or appropriate individual) containing the recommended:
    a. Improvement target and objective
    b. Annual milestones
    c. Improved or new systems and processes needed to realize the proposed target

Educational Uses of Benchmarking

Although almost any situation can be benchmarked, one needs to be fairly selective because this process can be expensive. Figure 4.17 suggests some potential educational situations warranting benchmarking.

Summary

Once a problem is in focus, it needs further analysis to both sharpen the picture and move the strategic thinking process into

LEVEL	POTENTIAL AREAS OF USE	SAMPLE USE
DISTRICT	• Full fledged benchmarking should be utilized in 3 to 5 areas of the district's (multiyear) plan annually. These should be the most critical areas and those which will create the most movement toward the district's vision. • On a smaller scale or more local/state or provincial scale, benchmarking might be used with any of the following: • Setting targets for attendance and recommending improvements in systems, procedures and processes which will create the most movement toward the proposed improvement target. • Setting a target for reducing the percentage of budget spent on administration (while increasing student scores on both standardized tests and other authentic measures). • Setting a target, procedures and processes for reducing student dropouts. • Setting a target for increasing business partnerships and/or external funding.	Review the scenario, Figure 4.15, and 4.16. and the directions on how to create or apply this tool. Having done so, you should be able to conceptually apply this tool to any or all of these potential uses.
SCHOOL	• Principal and teacher absenteeism. • Student test scores. • Student increased absences. • Funds raised by school. • Parent and community involvement. • Benchmark 3 to 5 key areas within the schools accreditation or strategic plan.	Review the scenario, Figure 4.15, and 4.16. and the directions on how to create or apply this tool. Having done so, you should be able to conceptually apply this tool to any or all of these potential uses.
CLASSROOM TEACHER	• Student absenteeism. • Student scores on standardized tests. • Parent community involvement. • Funds raised by class. • Students gaining recognition (academics, sports, arts, etc) • Students doing quality work.	Review the scenario, Figure 4.15, and 4.16. and the directions on how to create or apply this tool. Having done so, you should be able to conceptually apply this tool to any or all of these potential uses.
STUDENTS (within school and/or home)	• Any sport or extra curricular activity. • Being a best friend. • Being a well balanced student (school) son/daughter (home) and youth (self). • Percentage of brain utilized. • Body strength relative to size and weight.	Review the scenario, Figure 4.15, and 4.16. and the directions on how to create or apply this tool. Having done so, you should be able to conceptually apply this tool to any or all of these potential uses.

Figure 4.17. Educational Uses of Benchmarking at Various Levels

the beginning stages of planning and management. The seven newer quality tools facilitate the early planning stages of the problem-solving process. Several of the tools may be familiar to some educators (affinity diagrams, tree diagrams, matrix diagrams, and force-field analysis); other tools (interrelationship digraphs, radar diagrams, and benchmarking) represent unexplored quality tools for most. Of these new tools, benchmarking is a must for educators in pursuit of quality. Finding out who is considerably better at doing what you are doing, along with the "hows, whats, wheres, whys, and whens" of what contributes to the difference, is both valuable information and a healthy process to assist you in becoming better, perhaps even the best. When was the last time you rested in order to sharpen or acquire a tool for your educational toolbox?

Key Terms and Concepts

Affinity diagram. A creative group planning process that organizes brainstormed ideas into groupings based on their natural relationships as seen by the group.

Benchmarking. This is the process of identifying the very best in a particular class (world class), setting targets designed to motivate both you and your district to continue to improve until you eventually become better than the best.

Force-field analysis. This group planning process is used to identify the forces that either promote or inhibit change in a situation/problem and to identify potential solution strategies.

Interfacing. Coming together; joining to complement each other.

Interrelationship digraph. A planning tool that takes a central theme/idea/problem and maps out logical interrelationships in terms of cause and effect.

Linear responsibility guide. Often referred to as a linear responsibility chart, this guide diagrams who has the primary responsibility for completing each task along with who else needs to be involved, or informed, or updated.

Matrix. A chart that shows the relationships of several factors along one side of the chart so that they can be compared with other factors listed along another side of the chart. The prioritization matrix and linear responsibility charts are two examples of matrices.

Prioritization matrix. A chart used to prioritize alternative solution strategies using quality characteristics that may be weighted.

Radar/spider charts. Often referred to as spider or arachnid charts, this tool is used to record assessments. Each spoke radiating from the center of the wheel represents one of the measurement criteria utilized in the assessment.

Tree diagram. A planning tool used to logically and linearly chart out, in increasing detail, the various tasks that must be accomplished to complete a project or achieve a specific objective or goal.

References and Sources for Additional Reading

Camp, R. C. (1989). *Benchmarking: The search for industry best practices that lead to superior performance.* Milwaukee: ASQC Quality Press.

Collett, C., et al. (1992). *Managing daily management work.* Methuen, MA: GOAL/QPC.

Dickson, G., Doyle. S., & Latta, R. F. (1992). *Developing indicators and standards: Choosing appropriate measures and targets of educational performance.* Vancouver: B.C. Superintendent's Association.

GOAL/QPC. (1989). *Research report: Benchmarking.* Methuen, MA: Author.

Mizuno, S. (1988). *Management for quality improvement: The seven new QC tools.* Cambridge: Productivity Press.

Tucker, S., Oddo, F., & Brassard, M. (1993). *The educators' companion to the memory jogger plus: A resource guide for teaching & facilitating the seven management & planning tools.* Methuen, MA: GOAL/QPC.

(See also Bonstingl, Cartin, Johnson, Miller & Krumm, and 3 M Corporation in the Preface.)

✧ 5 ✧

Using Integrative Quality Tools:
Facilitating Planning and Management

*Only those who will risk going too far can possibly find out how
far they can go.*

T. S. ELIOT

Thus far we have discussed the group process quality tools, seven
basic quality tools for analyzing systems, and seven newer quality
tools for front-end planning. This chapter introduces four fairly
sophisticated integrative quality tools. These tools utilize a process
that coordinates many of the other quality tools in selecting a
solution strategy and designing a plan for guiding implementation,
monitoring, evaluation, and revision based upon feedback (the
CQI process). The four integrative quality tools discussed in this
chapter are action planning, activity networks, Plan-Do-Check-Act
(PDCA) cycles, and Hoshin planning (see Figure 5.1 for overview).

Action Planning

Understanding the What, Why, and How of Action Planning

SCENARIO: A group of students, coached by their teacher, use
quality tools (brainstorming, the focus group, fishbone diagrams,
interrelationship digraphs, force-field analysis, and benchmarking) to set an improvement target for significantly improving the
district's dropout rate. Their target is to reduce the district's rate

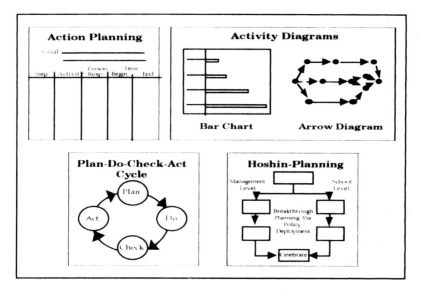

Figure 5.1. The Four Integrative Quality Tools

Note: These tools integrate many of the other quality tools presented in this text into their process.

from 29% to 7% over the next 5 years. (The superintendent and others are impressed, because this is almost identical to the improvement objective suggested by a previous group of adults who tackled the same problem.) The students then use matrix analysis and establish a flow tree as a prelude to action planning. Because they all consider themselves to be planning experts, the task becomes not one of action planning, but one of deciding what type of format to use for the planning scope sheets. The students produce three formats as illustrated in Figure 5.2.

Close to the end of the group session on action planning, the students break out laughing. "Isn't it silly to be fighting over formats when there is more important work to be done?" they ask, almost in unison.

"No," their teacher answers. "This is where most planning breaks down. Groups meet, discuss, and feel good about what

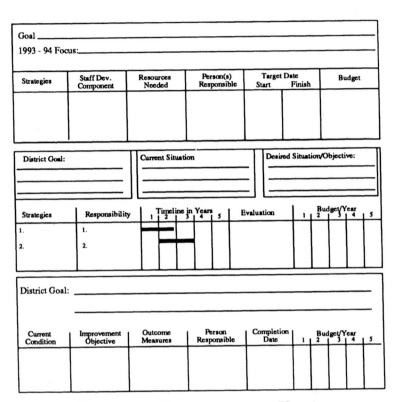

Figure 5.2. Three Sample Formats for Action Planning

they've accomplished, but nothing happens. There's no follow-up or follow-through." The teacher continues by adding that groups need to agree on a planning format, agree on who is doing what, and decide on the time schedule. Furthermore, the teacher emphasizes that people to whom responsibilities have been assigned must first agree to accept the responsibility, and the group must feel that these individuals possess the skills and have the commitment and time to meet their tasks on schedule.

What Is It?

Action planning is a process utilized by a group to identify the essential components of an improvement plan and to document these components in the form of a formal plan.

Why Use It?

Too often groups come together, make decisions, and nothing happens because there is no agreed-on plan of action. Participants also may not have agreed to accept responsibility for specific tasks. In many groups, if an action is put off long enough, it either disappears or someone else does it and there are no immediate consequences. The group action-planning process results in a formal improvement plan to which everyone is committed and united in completing. Group members are eager to be successful and look forward to the celebrations along the way.

How Do You Create It?

Group action planning is accomplished by the following steps:

1. Establish a representative group of six to eight people, most of whom have ownership in the problem and its resolution.

2. If problem analysis has been completed and an improvement objective established earlier via groups utilizing quality tools, then simply review the analysis data, validate the improvement objective, and move to the next step. If this has not been done, the group must utilize quality tools and establish a mutually agreed-on improvement objective. (Brainstorming, affinity diagrams, interrelationship digraphs, force-field analysis, and radar/spider charts help to analyze the problem and establish an improvement objective. If the problem is complex, benchmarking would be in order.)

3. Conduct an analysis of resources and constraints. (You may choose to use force-field analysis here.)

4. Identify alternative solutions to the problem and select the quality characteristics to be used in determining which of the potential solution strategies is the best.

5. Select the quality alternative solution that has the best chance of meeting the improvement objective. (You may choose to use matrix analysis here.)

6. Agree on a format for the improvement plan.

7. Identify and select activities for implementing the solution strategy. (A flowchart might be used here.)
8. List activities in the sequence they must be completed, along with the following for each activity:
   a. Person responsible
   b. Cost
   c. Resources needed
   d. Start date
   e. Completion date
   f. Evaluation (target/expected product or desired outcome)
9. Individuals in the group agree on responsibilities, time frame, resources needed, and product/outcome expected from them.
10. Complete the improvement plan by placing the specifics on the planning sheet previously selected and agreed on.
11. Everyone gets a copy of the plan developed and agreed on by the group.
12. Establish and agree on a schedule for meeting to discuss progress as well as assistance needed.
13. Individually and as a group, implement the improvement plan.

Educational Uses of the Action Planning Process

Figure 5.3 lists potential uses of the action planning process at various levels within education.

Activity Networks

Understanding the What, Why, and How of Activity Networks

SCENARIO: A representative group from the best school district in the world attends a workshop on Hoshin planning. Six months after the group returns to its district and utilizes this new quality tool, the district makes a phenomenal breakthrough. It not only meets its key annual target but also exceeds it by a considerable

Level	Potential Areas of Use	Sample Use
DISTRICT	Action planning can be used at the district level in conjunction with almost any of the quality tools discussed in this text as follows: • Those outlined in Brainstorming, Figure 2.2. • Those outlined in Pareto Charts, Figure 3.5. • Those outlined in Activity Networks, Figure 5.13. • Those outlined in Hoshin Planning, Figure 5.17. • Almost any district level improvement planning efforts. Note: Involving site administrators, teachers and students in district level use of this tool enhances the chances of their successfully using this tool at other levels.	Review the scenario, Figures 5.2 and the directions on how to create or apply this tool. Having done so, you should be able to conceptually apply this tool to any or all of these potential uses.
SCHOOL	Action planning can be used at the school level in conjunction with almost any of the quality tools discussed in this text as follows: • Those outlined in Brainstorming, Figure 2.2. • Those outlined in Pareto Charts, Figure 3.5. • Those outlined in Activity Networks, Figure 5.13. • Those outlined in Hoshin Planning, Figure 5.17. • Almost any school level improvement planning efforts. Note: Involving teachers, students and some parents in using this tool at the school level enhances the chances of their successfully using this tool at other levels.	Review the scenario, Figure 5.2 and the directions on how to create or apply this tool. Having done so, you should be able to conceptually apply this tool to any or all of these potential uses.
CLASSROOM TEACHER	Action planning can be used at the classroom level in conjunction with almost any of the quality tools discussed in this text as follows: • Those outlined in Brainstorming, Figure 2.2. • Those outlined in Pareto Charts, Figure 3.5. • Those outlined in Activity Networks, Figure 5.13. • Those outlined in Hoshin Planning, Figure 5.17. • Almost any classroom level improvement planning efforts. Note: Involving students and parents in using this tool at the school level enhances the chances of their successfully using this tool at other levels.	Review the scenario, Figure 5.2 and the directions on how to create or apply this tool. Having done so, you should be able to conceptually apply this tool to any or all of these potential uses.
STUDENTS (within school and/or home)	Action planning can be used at this level in conjunction with almost any of the quality tools discussed in this text as follows: • Those outlined in Brainstorming, Figure 2.2. • Those outlined in Pareto Charts, Figure 3.5. • Those outlined in Activity Networks, Figure 5.13. • Those outlined in Hoshin Planning, Figure 5.17. • Almost any youth initiated improvement planning efforts.	Review the scenario, Figure 5.2 and the directions on how to create or apply this tool. Having done so, you should be able to conceptually apply this tool to any or all of these potential uses.

Figure 5.3. Educational Uses of Action Planning at Various Levels

amount. It is time to celebrate. The same group that selected the priority problem, benchmarked the situation, and established the improvement objective, convenes once more to plan a celebration via an awards banquet. Everyone in the district will receive something special, and key people will receive additional forms of recognition. Members construct a flow tree diagram for the banquet (see Figure 5.4) and follow that with an arrow diagram, which is a form of activity network (see Figure 5.5). Both the group and the awards banquet are organized to the hilt.

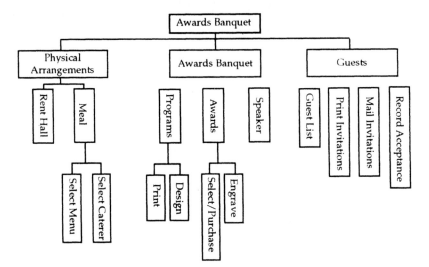

Figure 5.4. Flow Tree for Awards Banquet

What Is It?

An *activity network* is a model showing the tasks that need to be accomplished in order to get a job done, sequenced in the order they are to begin and to finish. These networks may also show beginning and completion dates, as well as estimates of the time required to accomplish each activity. Some networks are referred to as Gantt charts and others as arrow diagrams. Arrow diagrams are constructed to illustrate a more integrated network showing the interdependencies of the activities.

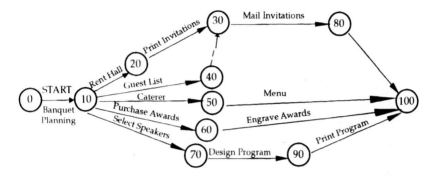

Figure 5.5. Arrow Diagram of Activities for Awards Banquet

Why Use It?

When time, costs, and quality are important factors, tasks related to the job must begin and finish in a specific sequence and in a timely fashion. For group members to work together effectively and efficiently, it helps for them to construct and share a model of the big picture that includes everything that needs to be completed and in what sequence. Looking at an activity network shows members where and how each contribution fits into the whole. They see and understand the consequences, should even one of them not hold up his or her end of the bargain. Further, in the event that an activity is behind schedule, other group members are more inclined to team up and help get things back on schedule.

How Do You Do It?

Because there are numerous techniques for establishing networks, it is important to select the best tool or technique for the project at hand. For simple to moderately complex projects, the bar chart or Gantt chart should be adequate. For more complex projects where activities are interdependent, an arrow diagram is a better choice.

A. The following steps are suggested for constructing and using a bar or Gantt chart:

1. Establish a representative group of four to six people who are both knowledgeable about the situation or project and will be involved in its implementation.

2. Have the group members brainstorm and identify all of the activities/tasks that must be undertaken and completed. The group might then construct an affinity diagram followed by a flowchart.

3. Develop a chart (see Figure 5.6) listing the activities on the left side in the order in which they must be undertaken to complete the project or resolve the problem. The task that must be undertaken first is placed at the top of the column, and the task that is to be completed last is placed at the bottom of the column.

4. Decide on the unit of time to be used (i.e., days, weeks, months, etc.) and develop a grid using this unit of time.

5. Estimate the time to complete each activity using the selected unit of time and construct a horizontal bar of the appropriate length for each activity on the grid.

6. Decide on a process for monitoring or charting the implementation of the project (see the legend, Figure 5.6).

7. Once the project is implemented, meet as per agreed-on schedule and update the status of each activity, using the previously agreed-on system.

8. Problem solve and focus attention on those activities behind schedule. As a team, continue to implement and complete the project as planned.

9. On completion, identify those things that need to be improved, should either this problem/solution or one similar to it be undertaken again, and make whatever changes/ improvements are necessary. (Each team member has learned from his or her experience and is now more empowered to continuously improve the processes relative to similar situations.)

10. The problem-solving team may choose to combine a linear responsibility guide with the bar chart (see Figure 5.7).

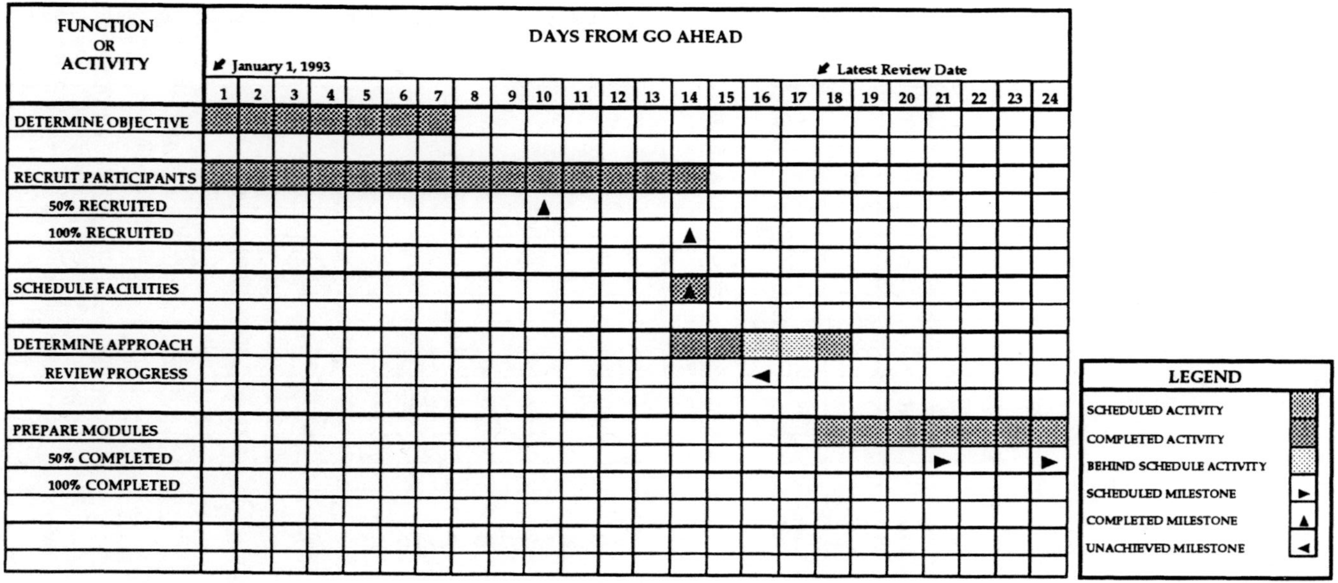

Figure 5.6. Function or Activity Time Chart

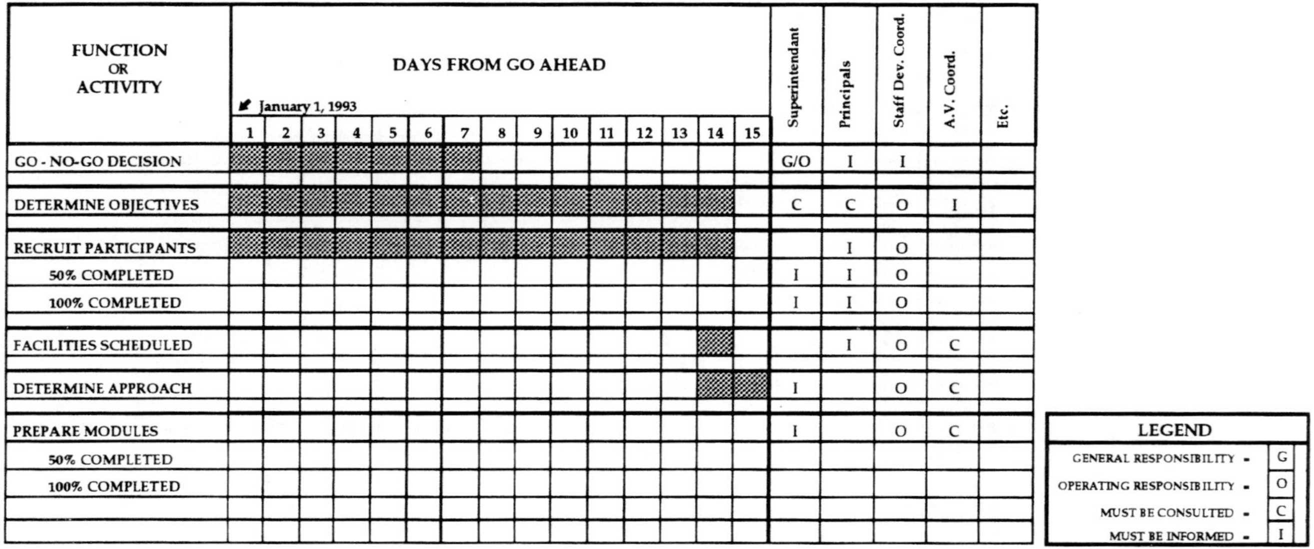

DAYS FROM GO AHEAD — January 1, 1993

FUNCTION OR ACTIVITY	1	2	3	4	5	6	7	8	9	10	11	12	13	14	15	Superintendant	Principals	Staff Dev. Coord.	A.V. Coord.	Etc.
GO - NO-GO DECISION	▓	▓	▓	▓	▓	▓	▓									G/O	I	I		
DETERMINE OBJECTIVES	▓	▓	▓	▓	▓	▓	▓	▓	▓	▓	▓	▓	▓	▓		C	C	O	I	
RECRUIT PARTICIPANTS	▓	▓	▓	▓	▓	▓	▓	▓	▓	▓	▓	▓	▓	▓		I	I	O		
50% COMPLETED																I	I	O		
100% COMPLETED																	I	O		
FACILITIES SCHEDULED														▓			I	O	C	
DETERMINE APPROACH														▓		I		O	C	
PREPARE MODULES																I		O	C	
50% COMPLETED																				
100% COMPLETED																				

LEGEND

GENERAL RESPONSIBILITY -	G
OPERATING RESPONSIBILITY -	O
MUST BE CONSULTED -	C
MUST BE INFORMED -	I

Figure 5.7. Combining a Bar Chart With a Linear Responsibility Guide

B. An arrow diagram is constructed using the following steps:

1. Establish a group/team of four to six people who are both knowledgeable about the project or problem situation and will be involved in its implementation. It is also a good idea to choose someone who is familiar with quality tools, particularly with constructing activity networks using arrow diagrams.

2. Have the group members brainstorm and identify all of the activities/tasks that must be completed either for the problem to be resolved or the project to be completed.

3. Decide whether an arrow diagram is the best tool for the job. This will be the case if you can respond yes to the following three questions:

    a. Does the project or problem have to be completed or resolved within a prescribed period of *time*?

    b. Are the activities interdependent with many things having to be done *concurrently*?

    c. Does the quality tool or technique utilized have to serve both as a good *communication tool* (show the big picture) as well as guide the *management* and *leadership functions* within the implementation process?

4. Construct an affinity diagram followed with a tree diagram.

5. Have two or three members of the group construct an arrow diagram using the principles and rules for establishing this type of network.

Arrow Diagram Principles and Rules

There are five principles and eleven network rules guiding the development of arrow diagrams.

A. The five guiding principles are

1. Establish critical milestone events and place them in their logical order prior to constructing a detailed network.

2. Establish the activity network using activities related to milestone events. Build the network from left (beginning)

to right (end) in order to construct a rough draft. Check the network by working back through it, right (end) to left (beginning). Designing the network from left to right should lead either to resolving the problem or meeting the project's objective(s). Checking the network, by working back through it, should end up at the beginning of the network.

3. Focus to facilitate project management and leadership pertaining to critical activities.

4. Regardless of how one constructs a network, the work flow during implementation is always left to right.

5. To solve a problem or complete a project, all activities must be completed. What may appear to be alternative paths are actually activities relating to other milestones that, while they may not be accomplished concurrently, must also be done.

B. The eleven network rules are:

1. An arrow indicates an activity or work that consumes time, money, or resources. Although the arrow represents the flow of time (left to right), its length has nothing to do with the amount of time or the difficulty of the work. Arrow diagrams are usually not drawn to scale.

2. An event is a completed activity and written about in the past tense. A number placed within a circle represents the event (Figure 5.8). The activity of designing and printing the invitations is placed over the activity arrow.

Figure 5.8. Illustration Showing the Difference Between Events and Activities

3. A broken or dotted line arrow represents a dummy activity and is used to connect completed activities back into the overall network at the appropriate place. All activities and corresponding events are connected within the overall network. There are no dead ends or loose ends in a network.

4. A double arrow represents the network's critical path or, in other words, the longest path through the network and thus the earliest point in time the project may be completed or the problem resolved.

5. An event or activity is unique and can only occur once in a network (Figure 5.9).

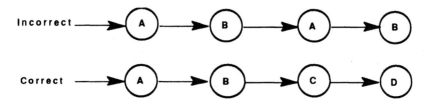

Figure 5.9. Correcting a Network Where an Event Occurs More Than Once

6. All work flow is left to right; therefore, looping back is impossible, as it is impossible to turn back time (Figure 5.10).

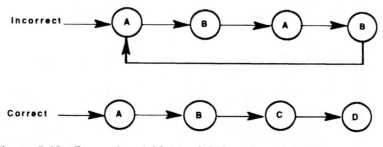

Figure 5.10. Correcting A Network Where Looping Was Attempted

7. Looping forward is also not permitted, as it both serves no purpose and is also confusing.

8. Two events cannot be connected by more than one activity (Figure 5.11).

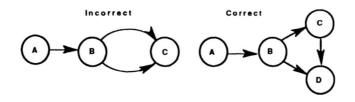

Figure 5.11. Correcting A Network With Two Events Connected by More Than One Activity

9. Paths in a network are identified by the events through which they pass. The arrow diagram in Figure 5.5 contains five paths as follows: 0, 10, 20, 30, 80, 100; 0, 10, 40, 30, 80, 100; 0, 10, 50, 100; 0, 10, 60, 100; and 0, 10, 70, 90, 100.

10. Events and activities serve as constraints on succeeding events and activities. For example, activity A-B cannot begin until event A has been completed (Figure 5.12).

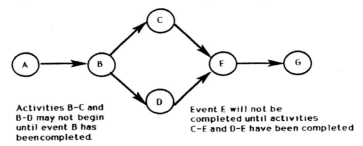

Figure 5.12. Network Showing How Events and Activities Serve as Constraints to Each Other

11. When the network has been completed, the events should be numbered as sequentially as possible, as was done in Figure 5.5.

Educational Uses of Activity Networks

Two tools for establishing activity networks are the bar or Gantt chart and the arrow diagram. The bar chart is the easier of the two to utilize and usually best for simple projects or problem-solving sequences. More complex action plans often call for a sophisticated tool like the arrow diagram. Regardless of the level of use (district, school, classroom, or home), educational stakeholders usually begin with the bar chart technique and branch into utilizing arrow diagrams. Figure 5.13 contains several uses of activity networks at various educational levels.

Plan-Do-Check-Act Cycle

Understanding the What, Why, and How of the Plan-Do-Check-Act Cycle

SCENARIO: Members of a focus group use quality tools to identify the district's most critical problem and establish an improvement objective with a specified target. They then meet with the superintendent who, being sensitive to the group, asks some members to join another group which will follow up on the focus group's work by developing an implementation and improvement plan for the problem identified. The improvement planning group consists of six people, four from the focus group and two new members. The members decide to use a Plan-Do-Check-Act (PDCA) cycle and integrate it with the action-planning process. Figure 5.14 illustrates the process followed by the planning group.

What Is It?

The *PDCA cycle* is a four-step planning process that, when complemented with full use of other quality tools, is a powerful group improvement planning tool.

Level	Potential Areas of Use	Sample Use
DISTRICT	Bar / Gantt Chart: • Preparing for and delivering a short workshop. • Planning a retirement party. • Writing a proposal for external funding. • Outlining the strategic planning process. Arrow Diagram: • Planning for district level accreditation. • Planning for passing a bond levy. • Planning to implement TQM. • Planning to implement the strategic planning process and the resultant plans. • Planning to construct a new school which will open on time. Note: Involving site personnel in using these tools at this level enhances the chances of their using them successfully at the school level.	Review the scenario, Figure 5.4, and the directions on how to create or apply this tool. Having done so, you should be able to conceptually apply this tool to any or all of these potential uses.
SCHOOL	Gantt / Bar Chart • Planning an orientation program for new teachers. • Planning for short workshops. • Planning to increase external funding. Arrow Diagram • Planning for a comprehensive track meet. • Preparing for school accreditation. • Planning for a comprehensive school carnival. • Plan for restructuring the school. • Plan for implementing outcome based education. Note: Involving staff and students in using these tools at this level enhances the chances of their using them successfully at the classroom level.	Review the scenario, Figure 5.4, and the directions on how to create or apply this tool. Having done so, you should be able to conceptually apply this tool to any or all of these potential uses.
CLASSROOM TEACHER	Bar/Gantt charts and/or Arrow Diagrams: • Planning to eliminate students showing up late to class. • Planning to eliminate discipline problems. • Planning to triple funds raised via external sources. • Planning to convert a traditional classroom into one which is ungraded. • Planning which would result in all students assuming a greater responsibility for their own learning. Note: Involving students in using these tools within the classroom is critical to their successfully utilizing them at home and/or in their private lives.	Review the scenario, Figure 5.5, and the directions on how to create or apply this tool. Having done so, you should be able to conceptually apply this tool to any or all of these potential uses.
STUDENTS (within school and/or home)	Bar / Gantt charts and/or Arrow Diagrams: • Planning related to doing an assignment or a term paper. • Planning related to purchasing a second hand automobile. • Planning related to finding either a summer or a part time job. • Planning related to getting room cleaned and chores completed earlier rather than later.	Review the scenario, Figure 5.5, and the directions on how to create or apply this tool. Having done so, you should be able to conceptually apply this tool to any or all of these potential uses.

Figure 5.13. Educational Uses of Activity Diagrams at Various Levels

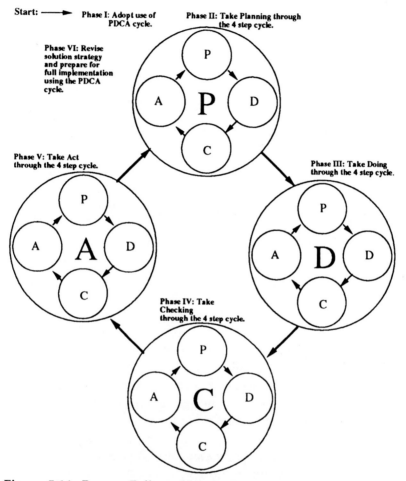

Figure 5.14. Process Followed by the District Improvement Planning Team (Pilot Testing a Solution Strategy)

Why Use It?

The phrase, "plan, do, check, act," is friendly, easily under-stood, and motivates people to join in and utilize it as a planning and management tool. The cycle is also easy to use and draws on almost all of the quality tools discussed in this book. It can be used with even the simplest of problems or, for more complex issues, to provide groups with an easily understood process for tackling unfamiliar or unfriendly situations.

How Do You Create It?

The PDCA cycle involves the following steps:

1. Establish a representative group of six to eight people, most of whom are familiar with the problem area and one or two of whom are familiar with quality tools, including this process.
2. After identifying the problem, match the complexity/depth of the improvement planning process with the problem. (Remember, there is a right tool for every job, and no one appreciates making a situation more complex than it need be.)
3. For relatively simple problems, the group may integrate a simplified form of action planning at each step of the cycle, utilizing one or two quality tools as needed throughout the cycle:
   a. PLAN. What is the problem? What changes are desired? What is the improvement target and objective? What resources are available? Collect and analyze data. Develop an improvement plan using the action-planning process.
   b. DO. Implement and monitor the improvement plan. Keep data needed to check/evaluate progress against the baseline data. Make minor adjustments as needed.
   c. CHECK. Determine progress that has been made toward the improvement target/objective. Note other ramifications or ripple effects that have been caused by implementing this particular solution strategy. Document what has been learned about the supporting systems, procedures, and processes.
   d. ACT. Decide together to abandon the improvement strategy, modify it, strengthen it, or continue without modification.
   e. PLAN. Update the plan based on what was learned during the first full cycle and then continue the cycle.

For complex problems, the group needs to be more rigorous and formal with each step of the PDCA cycle. For example, many quality tools may have to be utilized and a separate action plan developed for each stage: planning, doing or implementing, checking or evaluating, and acting or decision making (see Figure 5.14). Solutions to complex problems should be field tested on a small-scale basis prior to full implementation.

Educational Uses of the PDCA Cycle

The PDCA cycle can be applied to solve any problem. Figure 5.15 lists potential educational uses of the cycle at various levels.

Hoshin Planning

Understanding the What, Why, and How of Hoshin Planning

SCENARIO: A district, which has long thought it is the best at offering a world-class education to all students, wakes up one day to realize its drop-out rate is 7%. A representative group begins to study the gnawing issue of no longer being the best, and members decide to attend a workshop on Hoshin planning. Toward the end of the workshop, they participate in a synthesizer exercise in which small groups bring aspects of Hoshin planning (or policy deployment) together to develop a model of the process (Figure 5.16). They decide to discuss their model in a more informal environment, so they go to a nearby coffee shop. The conversation is about Hoshin philosophy: Keep things simple; focus on one thing; if you cannot do one thing well, you have no chance of doing a great many things well; big ideas scare some people; turn organizations into centers of continual learning; and along with the deployment of function, method, action and responsibility must also go the deployment of credit, glory, limelight, permission, and resources.

LEVEL	POTENTIAL AREAS OF USE	SAMPLE USE
DISTRICT	• Plan, implement and evaluate a system for constructing and opening a new school on schedule. • Plan, implement and evaluate a charter school. • Convert a junior high school to a middle school. • Up-date system and procedures for hiring and retiring a certified and classified staff. • Implementing district's strategic plan. • Translating the TQM philosophy and practice to a Total Quality Education (TQE) practice. • Designing a program(s) which ensure that 100% of the students in the school are successful. • Implementing a "world class" parent education and involvement program. • Becoming the "number one" school district in the state or province. • Reducing administrative costs / expenditures in the district by 50%. Note: Involving site administrators and teachers in district level use of this tool enhances the chances of their using it successfully at the school level.	Review the scenario, Figure 5.14. and the directions on how to create or apply this tool. Having done so, you should be able to conceptually apply this tool to any or all of these potential uses.
SCHOOL	• Identifying and establishing new partnerships designed to garner additional money, resources and personnel. • Identify, select, implement, monitor and evaluate new uses of technology to compliment teachers' instruction and to ensure all students success in learning. • Identify and implement new strategies for utilizing paraprofessionals in learning situations, particularly: high school and college students; business personnel; and retirees, particularly retired educators; etc. • Plan, implement, monitor and evaluate a new school within a school program. • Restructure a school into a learning enterprise system. • Institute a TQM system in the school which results in a Total Quality Education (TQE) system. Note: Involving all teachers, and some students in using this tool at the school level enhances the chances of teachers successfully using this tool within their classroom.	Review the scenario, Figure 5.14. and the directions on how to create or apply this tool. Having done so, you should be able to conceptually apply this tool to any or all of these potential uses.
CLASSROOM TEACHER	• Plan, implement, monitor, evaluate and continuously strengthen a mastery learning system in math and spelling. • Plan, implement, monitor, evaluate and continuously improve a system which ensures that all students are successfully learning at or above grade level. • Plan, and implement a system designed to ensure that all homework is understood before going home and successfully completed and turned in on time. • Plan and implement a system which continues to strengthen the classroom climate and the self-esteem of all the students. • Plan and implement a system which excites adults, parents, etc., to assist in the learning process such that each month the adult/student ratio is increasing to the desired level of 1:4. Note: Involving all students and some parents in using this tool at the classroom level enhances the chances of student successfully using this tool in both their private and home life.	Review the scenario, Figure 5.4. and 5.14, and the directions on how to create or apply this tool. Having done so, you should be able to conceptually apply this tool to any or all of these potential uses.
STUDENTS (within school and/or home)	• Plan and implement a system designed to improve one's GPA from a C plus to a B plus within a six month period of time. • Plan and implement a system designed to minimize learning loss over the summer vacation while doubling this summer's income over last. • Having secured a summer or part time job, the PDCA cycle might be useful in both doing the job as currently designed and assisting the owner/manager in redesigning it within the spirit of continuous improvement.	Review the scenario, Figure 5.4. and 5.14, and the directions on how to create or apply this tool. Having done so, you should be able to conceptually apply this tool to any or all of these potential uses.

Figure 5.15. Educational Uses of the PDCA Cycle at Various Levels

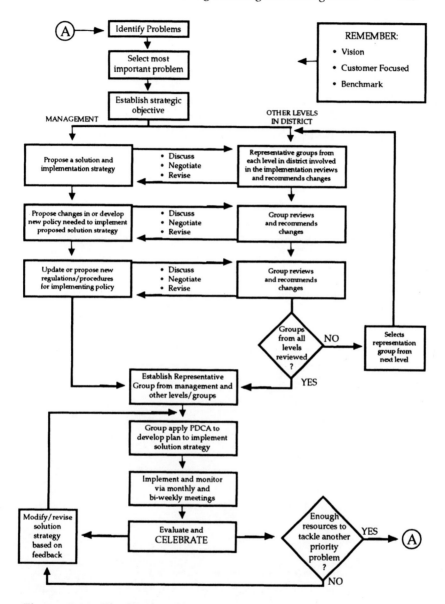

Figure 5.16. The Hoshin Planning Process

What Is It?

Hoshin planning is a philosophy based on doing the one thing that will create the most movement towards your vision or improvement objective. *Hoshin* is a Chinese word for "shiny metal object showing direction," or a compass, something that guides one along the best pathway to a vision or journey. Although the Japanese call this process Hoshin planning, in the United States it is referred to as policy deployment.

Why Use It?

Think about the concepts in the following questions:

1. Is it better to do one high priority thing right the first time or do numerous low priority things right?
2. Would you rather be proactive and empower and excite everyone in your district or be reactive and continue to do "more of the same"?
3. Would you rather create a community of learners and leaders or live with doing things tomorrow the way they were done today and have always been done?

The former part of each of the three questions is basic to Hoshin planning. The latter part represents the way most things are done in education today. If your intent is to translate a customer-focused vision into action, Hoshin planning is an essential quality tool. It is critical to CQI and TQE.

How Do You Do It?

Hoshin planning principles may be used either within a district that desires to embark upon quality improvement planning in the absence of a strategic plan or, much more powerfully, within a district that has completed or is going through the strategic planning process. Although the steps may vary somewhat within the two uses, they are as follows:

1. Establish a customer-focused vision via the input and involvement of representatives from all stakeholder groups.
2. Establish a focus group to identify, analyze, and select one or two top priority problems that are solvable.
3. Take the one or two problems and benchmark them.
4. Analyze alternative solutions that hold potential in meeting established targets and improvement objectives.
5. Review the district's policies relating to the problems and solution strategies, and examine district procedures and regulations for implementing them.
6. Bring together management and teams from various levels within the district to implement the solution strategy. Facilitate them in a catch-ball process in which managers meet with representatives (principals, teachers, etc.) from various levels to discuss targets, solution strategies, and policies and regulations for implementing them. The principals may say that the solutions will not work because of a few key reasons and suggest some changes. The management group considers the input and makes revisions, and the two groups interact again and again, as necessary. When this is completed, the management representatives meet with a group of representatives from the next level, perhaps teachers, and the process of sharing, communicating, and negotiating continues. The process continues until representatives from all levels have been involved. The initiating/facilitating group members then revise the improvement targets, improvement or strategic objectives, solution strategies, and policies and accompanying regulations and procedures.
7. Take what has been learned, and use the new knowledge within an action-planning process or PDCA process in order to develop an action plan. Definitely do a 1-year plan, and, if there is interest, a multiyear plan.
8. Establish biweekly and monthly meeting dates. Progress is reviewed by examining biweekly and/or monthly subtargets established within the benchmarking process.

9. Implement and monitor the improvement plan via bi-weekly and monthly meetings.

10. Always look for situations that warrant celebrating.

11. Make changes when and where necessary. Solve problems as they occur during the journey rather than at the end of the road.

12. Continue the PDCA process. Hoshin planning maintains this focus until the improvement targets have been met. No new thrusts are begun until a breakthrough has been accomplished and/or the targets met. (Another problem may be tackled if a school system finds it has adequate resources to take on another priority problem using Hoshin principles.)

In summary, the keys to Hoshin planning or policy deployment are:

- A customer-focused vision
- Simplicity (focus on one or two critical problems or strategies)
- Continuous improvement (use the PDCA cycle)
- Involvement of others
- Communication

Educational Uses of Hoshin Planning

The principles and concepts of Hoshin planning can be useful in any educational problem-solving or decision-making effort. Figure 5.17 illustrates potential educational uses of Hoshin planning at various levels.

Summary

Educators have made little use of the integrative quality tools (action planning, activity networks, the PDCA cycle, and Hoshin planning), except perhaps for action planning. Many erroneously believe that using a particular tool or label will, like magic, solve

LEVEL	POTENTIAL AREAS OF USE	SAMPLE USE
DISTRICT	• Use to focus on the single most important strategic direction or objective with a district's strategic plan. As most district strategic plans include anywhere from six to twenty strategic directions, this process narrows a district's efforts down to the 'one' critical achievement, that when successfully met / resolved, will create the most movement towards a district's positive vision of its future. • The process may be utilized to create movement in areas where programs has been stalled for one or more years and where long standing policies must be changed for movement to occur, for example • Reduce / Eliminate student dropout. • Reduce tension between the board and teachers' association. • Reduce class size. • Move to year round schedule. • Changing personnel evaluation systems and procedures.	Review the scenario, Figure 5.16. and the directions on how to create or apply this tool. Having done so, you should be able to conceptually apply this tool to any or all of these potential uses.
SCHOOL	• Use to focus on the single most important strategy / objective with a school's strategic and / or accreditation multi-year plan. Most school accreditation processes result in ten - to twenty general objectives to be achieved with a five or six year time period. This process narrows the school's year to 'one' critical achievement, that when successfully met /resolved, creates the most movement towards the school's positive vision of its future. • The process may be utilized to create movement in areas where progress has been stalled for several years and where long standing policies must be changed for movement to occur, for example • Student grading and reporting of grades. • Student behavior and dress code. • Moving to mastery learning. • Moving to Outcomes Based Education. • Moving to school based strategic planning with a focus on continuous quality improvement. • Defining what constitutes unacceptable, acceptable, and exceptional teaching.	Review the scenario, Figure 5.16. and the directions on how to create or apply this tool. Having done so, you should be able to conceptually apply this tool to any or all of these potential uses.
CLASSROOM TEACHER	• Revise and / or develop a code for classroom behavior and discipline. • Selecting, using and evaluating para-professionals in the classroom. • Job sharing with another teacher. • Doing an internship / exchange with someone in business. • Benchmarking one's class using the process outlined for benchmarking in this text.	Review the scenario, Figure 5.16. and the directions on how to create or apply this tool. Having done so, you should be able to conceptually apply this tool to any or all of these potential uses.
STUDENTS (within school and / or home)	• Reviewing and / or establishing curfew. • Reviewing and / or establishing transportation challenges or problems. • Establishing a solution to the challenge of improving both one's GPA and weekly income. • Reviewing and changing any home or school situation where long standing policies or practices are holding the situation in a steady state.	Review the scenario, Figure 5.16. and the directions on how to create or apply this tool. Having done so, you should be able to conceptually apply this tool to any or all of these potential uses.

Figure 5.17. Educational Uses of Hoshin Planning at Various Levels

all their problems. They may not be aware that action planning is usually ineffective when used in the absence of other quality tools. However, it can serve a purpose when applied to relatively simple problems. In this way, educators can learn how to utilize action plans as preparation for implementing them within a group process along with other quality tools.

The remaining three integrative quality tools are strangers to most educators, even though there has been some dabbling around the edges of two of the tools (activity networks and the PDCA cycle). Action planning and the PDCA cycle will probably be used more than the other two integrative quality tools because they are the most basic. Activity networks and Hoshin planning are likely to be used at the district level and for solving more complex problems.

The fact that few educators have made use of the four integrative quality tools does not mean that these processes are of little value or that they are difficult to learn or use. One can only judge their true value in education's journey toward quality by using the tools firsthand.

Key Terms and Concepts

Action planning. A group process that identifies essential components (tasks, processes, systems, etc.) and logically sequences them as a formal quality improvement plan.

Activity network. A diagram showing the activities that need to be accomplished to get a job completed within a specific time period. The activities are sequenced in the order in which they need to both begin and be completed.

Arrow diagram. This planning tool produces a detailed network linking events (completed activities) with flow arrows. The arrows represent activities, their sequence, and when they begin and end. These networks can be made much more complete and complex than those illustrated in this text.

Bar chart. Often referred to as a Gantt chart, this represents activities (horizontally) and the sequence in which they are to begin (vertically from the top of the chart to the bottom).

Breakthrough thinking. A method of problem solving designed to cause people to think in nontraditional ways that create new and creative solutions to problems.

Gantt chart. See bar chart.

Hoshin planning. A system of planning, also referred to as policy deployment, designed to create significant breakthroughs. Most school districts and schools plan so many things that often little is accomplished. Hoshin planning is based on identifying the one thing that, if accomplished, will create the most movement toward a vision. The energy, enthusiasm, and excitement needed to continue the journey towards CQI is thereby created throughout the entire system.

Integrative quality tools. These are processes, themselves interdependent upon numerous other quality tools, that facilitate action planning and exemplify CQI as a dynamic learning and growing process.

Plan-Do-Check-Act (PDCA) cycle. This tool is a cycle consisting of four major steps: plan, do, check, and act. Each of the major steps consists of the same four microsteps: plan, do, check, act.

Policy deployment. See Hoshin planning.

Vision. A brief, powerful impact statement of a desired future made by a school district or school.

Strategic planning. A process by which an organization envisions its future and develops the necessary systems, procedures, and operations to achieve its vision.

System. A group of interdependent parts working together as a whole to meet organizational goals.

References and Sources for Additional Reading

GOAL/QPC. (1989). *Research report: Hoshin planning.* Methuen, MA: Author.

King, R. (1989). *Hoshin planning: The developmental approach.* Methuen, MA: GOAL/QPC.

Latta, R. F., & Matheson, R. (1992). *Preparing for the future: Making strategic thinking, strategic leadership, and renewal part of everyday life into the twenty-first century.* Vancouver: B.C. Superintendent's Association.

Nadler, G., & Hibino, S. (1990). *Breakthrough thinking: Why we must change the way we solve problems, and the seven principles to achieve this.* Rocklin, CA: Prima Publishing & Communications.

Scholtes, P. R., et al. (1988). *The team handbook: How to improve quality with teams.* Madison, WI: Joiner Associates.

(See also Bonstingl, Cartin, Johnson, and 3 M Corporation in the Preface.)

✧ 6 ✧

Empowering Educational Stakeholders
to Use Quality Tools

> *Do not go*
> *where the path*
> *may lead,*
> *go instead*
> *where there is no path*
> *and leave a trail.*
>
> EMERSON

Where To Begin?

Change may be slow in education, but *slow* does not necessarily imply *bad*. An effort as all-encompassing as supporting a paradigm shift, however, may take a great deal of time. In Table 6.1 we demonstrate the shifts in thinking that are necessary in order to reap the benefits promised by CQI.

Paradigm shifts begin at the top. They are most likely when superintendents and boards make visible long-term commitments to CQI and when there is adequate human resource training available to make a commitment systemic. Leaders at all levels must walk their talk. If principals and teachers desire to implement CQI, they must model the use of the quality tools for their colleagues, instructional and support staff, students and parents. The most desired situation, of course, is to begin at the district level, but any educational stakeholder can initiate CQI. Waiting around for someone else to start is cowardly thinking—all educators can begin right now.

TABLE 6.1 Paradigm Shift Prerequisites for CQI

Old Thinking	Thinking for CQI
A. Continuously improve what has always been done (i.e., do "more of the same").	Continuous Quality Improvement changes for the better what needs improving relative to improving quality.
B. Variance in our schools is to be expected. We are doing the best we can with the existing resources.	Continuously reduce variance by redesigning systems and establishing better priorities for allocating existing resources.
C. Education has few similarities with business. The last thing we should consider is to adopt business tools/techniques or practices.	Education is sufficiently similar to business for us to adapt those business tools, techniques, and practices holding promise in assisting us to continuously improve the quality of education.
D. Problem solving should be done mainly by those who will be responsible for implementing the selected solution strategies.	Problem solving should utilize cross-functional groups wherever possible, thus enriching the creativity of the group.
E. Education has very few tools of the trade. Most tools should, and do, deal with teaching.	Education has a great many tools of the trade. Many relate to planning for CQI and others help ensure that all students are successful learners now and throughout the future.

Suppose we consider an example of why taxpayers and politicians tend to be skeptical about educators' ability to change, do what is right for kids, and do it right now. One of the simplest forms of technology, the microcomputer, came onto the educational scene in the mid-1970s. There it was: a tremendous learning tool, one that could be used by children in ways totally inconceivable to those adults whose creativity had been stifled by the same educational system they continued to perpetuate. Almost 20 years have passed and both schools and educators have underutilized this tool that could have delivered so much.

In this volume we have illustrated how CQI tools help educators establish baseline data; focus on real problems; develop, implement, and monitor progress; evaluate actions taken; and continuously improve the situation (see Figure 6.1).

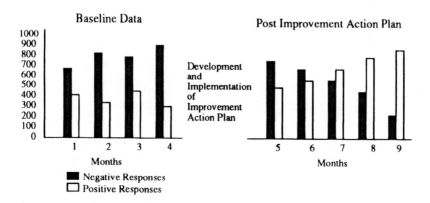

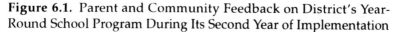

Figure 6.1. Parent and Community Feedback on District's Year-Round School Program During Its Second Year of Implementation

Note: The continuous decrease of negative and increase of positive responses from the 5th month through the 9th month is an excellent example of continuous improvement.

Must CQI and quality tools wait 20 years more before a glimpse of progress in education is seen? Business is well into CQI philosophy, principles, practices, and tools already, and the rewards gained from the pursuit of quality outside education have been staggering, to say the least. Changes occur almost overnight as businesses totally restructure to improve quality, do more with less, and increase their competitiveness. In addition, parents and children increasingly are using tools at home to improve the quality of their lives. In short, they are learning what quality is and how to attain it.

We believe that educators in the public school system must move into CQI within 2 to 3 years or face the possibility of being quickly swallowed up by private school systems. The public at large will not wait 20 years for quality to become the norm in public education. From our perspective, the only choices are to wait, be reactive, and perhaps lose what little credibility the public school system still has or get started now, be proactive, and work to regain the public's confidence.

The CQI movement has already begun without education and is well under way in the larger "learning" community. We urge you to begin the CQI process *today* with yourself at whatever level you serve within the educational system.

Strategies for Using Quality Tools, Techniques, and Processes

A quick reference to Figure 1.4 shows where each quality tool might be utilized within the problem-solving process. Quality tools may be used on a *stand-alone* basis to reduce variance and thus continuously improve quality, or along with other quality tools. For example, to identify a specific problem, one might utilize as many as six quality tools, either in sequence or concurrently, within a particular process.

Another way to examine how, where, when, and why to utilize quality tools for CQI is to consider their use within the PDCA cycle (see Figure 6.2 as one example). With practice, you will likely gravitate toward using somewhere between five and ten of the quality tools most consistent with your style of thinking.

Regardless of which tools you prefer, remember to introduce new users to a wide variety of quality tools so they can discover the ones most consistent with their own style. A good stretch exercise is to learn and utilize at least one new quality tool each year that is not aligned with your thinking and learning style. Even if practice does not lead to perfection, it will lead to CQI.

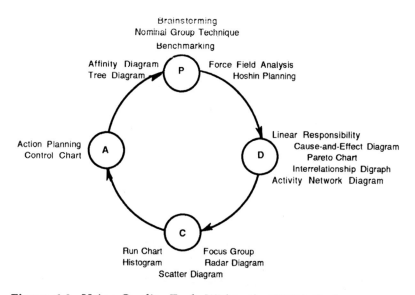

Brainstorming
Nominal Group Technique
Benchmarking

Affinity Diagram
Tree Diagram

P

Force Field Analysis
Hoshin Planning

Action Planning
Control Chart

A

D

Linear Responsibility
Cause-and-Effect Diagram
Pareto Chart
Interrelationship Digraph
Activity Network Diagram

C

Run Chart
Histogram

Focus Group
Radar Diagram

Scatter Diagram

Figure 6.2. Using Quality Tools Within the PDCA Cycle

Beginning Right Now

CQI will succeed where the commitment, philosophy, and tools become a visible, meaningful part of everyday life—the accepted norm throughout the educational profession. All sectors must be equipped to partner a broader learning community with educational leaders.

According to an African proverb, it takes a whole village to raise a child. Likewise, it takes a united community to educate our nation's children. It is the continuous pursuit of quality that might provide the unity needed to create such a community. It begins with you, with me, and with us.

Shall we leave the familiar path and risk venturing wholeheartedly into the quality way of life? Given the depth of the trench that we educators have dug for ourselves, it will take an entire community with a new spirit and commitment to move the educational system to the center of the quality movement. We must all move both feet forward and, right now, dare to blaze a new trail.

References and Sources for Additional Reading

Belasco, J. A., & Stayer, R. C. (1993). *Flight of the buffalo: Soaring to excellence, learning to let employees lead.* New York: Warner Books.

Crosby, P. B. (1990). *The eternally successful organization.* New York: New American Library.

Depree, M. (1989). *Leadership is an art.* New York: Doubleday.

Juran, J. M. (1989). *Juran on leadership for quality: An executive handbook.* New York: Free Press.

Kinlaw, D. C. (1989). *Coaching for commitment: Managerial strategies for obtaining superior performance.* San Diego: Pfeiffer & Company.

Kinlaw, D. C. (1990). *Developing superior work teams: Building quality and the competitive edge.* New York: Free Press.

Richardson,, B., & Fusco, M. A. (1993). *The 10% principle: How to get extraordinary results from ordinary people.* San Diego: Pfeiffer & Company.

Ryan, K. D., & Oestreich, D. K. (1991). *Driving fear out of the workplace.* San Francisco: Jossey-Bass.

Wick, C. W., & Leon, L. S. (1993). *The learning edge: How smart managers and smart companies stay ahead.* New York: McGraw-Hill.

✧   ✧

Planning and Troubleshooting Guide